WORLD RELIGIONS

CATHOLICISM

& ORTHODOX CHRISTIANITY

THIRD EDITION

WORLD RELIGIONS

African Traditional Religion
Baha'i Faith
Buddhism
Catholicism & Orthodox Christianity
Confucianism
Daoism
Hinduism
Islam
Judaism
Native American Religions
Protestantism
Shinto
Sikhism
Zoroastrianism

WORLD RELIGIONS
CATHOLICISM
& ORTHODOX CHRISTIANITY
THIRD EDITION

by **CENTRAL**

Stephen F. Brown and Khaled Anatolios
Series Editors: Joanne O'Brien and Martin Palmer

CHELSEA HOUSE
PUBLISHERS
An imprint of Infobase Publishing

Catholicism & Orthodox Christianity, Third Edition

Chelsea House
An imprint of Infobase Publishing
132 West 31st Street
New York NY 10001

Library of Congress Cataloging-in-Publication Data
Brown, Stephen F.
 Catholicism & Orthodox Christianity / by Stephen F. Brown and Khaled Anatolios. — 3rd ed.
    p. cm. — (World religions)
 Includes bibliographical references and index.
 ISBN 978-1-60413-106-2 (alk. paper)
 1. Orthodox Eastern Church—Relations—Catholic Church—History. 2. Catholic Church—Relations—Orthodox Eastern Church—History. I. Anatolios, Khaled, 1962- II. Title. III. Title: Catholicism and Orthodox Christianity. IV. Series.

 BX324.3.B76 2009
 280'.209—dc22

                    2008043046

Chelsea House books are available at special discounts when purchased in bulk quantities for businesses, associations, institutions, or sales promotions. Please call our Special Sales Department in New York at (212) 967-8800 or (800) 322-8755.

You can find Chelsea House on the World Wide Web at http://www.chelseahouse.com

This book was produced for Chelsea House by Bender Richardson White, Uxbridge, U.K.
Project Editor: Lionel Bender
Text Editor: Ronne Randall
Designer: Ben White
Picture Researchers: Joanne O'Brien and Kim Richardson
Maps and symbols: Stefan Chabluk

Printed in China

CP BRW 10 9 8 7 6 5 4 3 2 1

This book is printed on acid-free paper.

All links and Web addresses were checked and verified to be correct at the time of publication. Because of the dynamic nature of the Web, some addresses and links may have changed since publication and may no longer be valid.

CONTENTS

PREFACE

Almost from the start of civilization, more than 10,000 years ago, religion has shaped human history. Today more than half the world's population practice a major religion or indigenous spiritual tradition. In many 21st-century societies, including the United States, religion still shapes people's lives and plays a key role in politics and culture. And in societies throughout the world increasing ethnic and cultural diversity has led to a variety of religions being practiced side by side. This makes it vital that we understand as much as we can about the world's religions.

The World Religions series, of which this book is a part, sets out to achieve this aim. It is written and designed to appeal to both students and general readers. The books offer clear, accessible overviews of the major religious traditions and institutions of our time. Each volume in the series describes where a particular religion is practiced, its origins and history, its central beliefs and important rituals, and its contributions to world civilization. Carefully chosen photographs complement the text, and sidebars, a map, fact file, glossary, bibliography, and index are included to help readers gain a more complete understanding of the subject at hand.

These books will help clarify what religion is all about and reveal both the similarities and differences in the great spiritual traditions practiced around the world today.

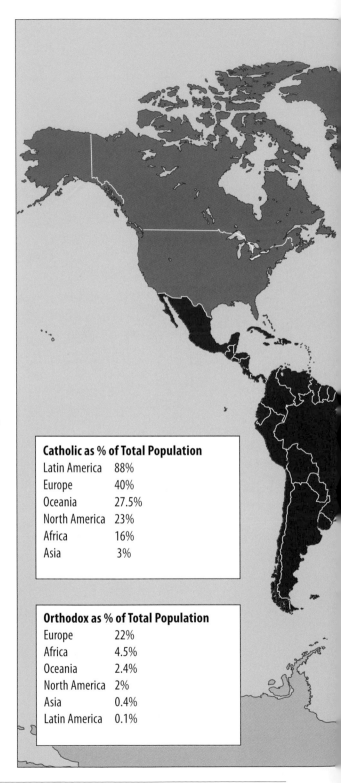

Catholic as % of Total Population

Latin America	88%
Europe	40%
Oceania	27.5%
North America	23%
Africa	16%
Asia	3%

Orthodox as % of Total Population

Europe	22%
Africa	4.5%
Oceania	2.4%
North America	2%
Asia	0.4%
Latin America	0.1%

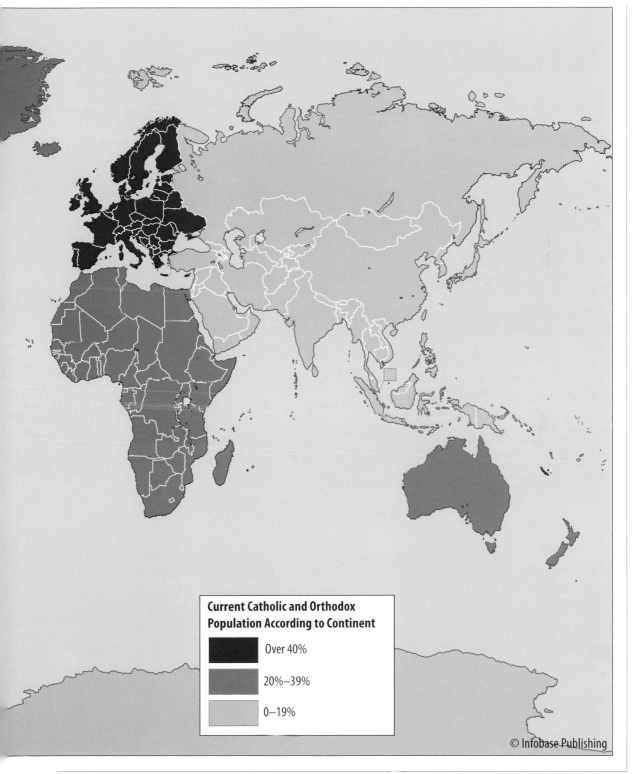

**Current Catholic and Orthodox
Population According to Continent**

Over 40%

20%–39%

0–19%

© Infobase Publishing

CHAPTER 1

INTRODUCTION: THE MODERN CATHOLIC AND ORTHODOX WORLDS

When Americans think of Christianity, they generally think of Protestantism or Roman Catholicism. Unless they have grown up in an Orthodox community, they will probably not be so aware of the Orthodox Church.

In the media we often see the pope at a grand ceremony greeting young people, or blessing the sick. We are used to seeing Protestant pastors on television, and often they are active in local community affairs as well. The same is true for the Orthodox churches. They too have world leaders who draw huge crowds, care for the sick, preach, appear on television, and are active locally.

CATHOLIC CHURCHES IN AMERICA

Catholicism has influenced the lives of Americans in many ways. Catholic schools in America have educated millions of citizens,

Saint Peter's Basilica in Saint Peter's Square, Vatican City. The Catholic Church is centered on the Vatican, a self-governing city-state in Rome. There are 1.1 billion Catholics worldwide served by more than 4.2 million people engaged in pastoral activity.

and Catholic hospitals have cared for millions of patients. Catholic charities have served the poor and sheltered the homeless. With other Christian churches, the Catholic Church has celebrated America's most festive holiday, Christmas. It has also added particular Catholic celebrations: Saint Patrick's Day in Irish neighborhoods; Saint Anthony's Feast in Italian districts; Saint Barbara's Feast in Eastern Catholic parishes with links to the Near East; and Saint Lazarus Saturday, with its processions in Syrian and Lebanese communities on the eve of Palm Sunday. John F. Kennedy was the first Catholic president. In all facets of American life, Catholics have played a large part.

Catholics have also brought a great deal of diversity to American life, place names, and architecture. If you drive around American cities, you might find Roman Catholic churches named after Saint Ludwig (German), Saint Brendan (Irish), Saint Louis (French), Saint Stephen (Hungarian), Saint Theresa of Avila (Spanish), Saint Bartholomew (Armenian), or Saint Charbel (Maronites, especially from Lebanon).

ORTHODOX CHURCHES IN AMERICA

The first Orthodox church on the American continent was established in 1792 on Kodiak Island, in present-day Alaska, by eight monks from western Russia. The Russian Orthodox Church is unique among major religious groups in the United States: It is the only church to expand from west to east. It moved its original headquarters from Sitka, Alaska, to San Francisco, then to New York City. The Church of Saint Nicholas, built in 1901 in New York City, became the main Russian Orthodox church in the United States in 1905.

There were at that time about 20,000 Russian Orthodox members in 60 parishes throughout the United States, but within a decade the numbers had grown to 100,000 with 169 parishes, and by 1975 there were more than a million parishioners. The Greek Orthodox Church established itself toward the end of the 19th century in the large cities of New York and Chicago and fanned out to other regions, having more than 2 million mem-

Saint Patrick's Cathedral, with its neo-Gothic spires, nestles among the skyscrapers of Manhattan in New York City. Opened in 1879, Saint Patrick's is the largest Gothic-style cathedral in the United States and a leading center of Catholic life in the country.

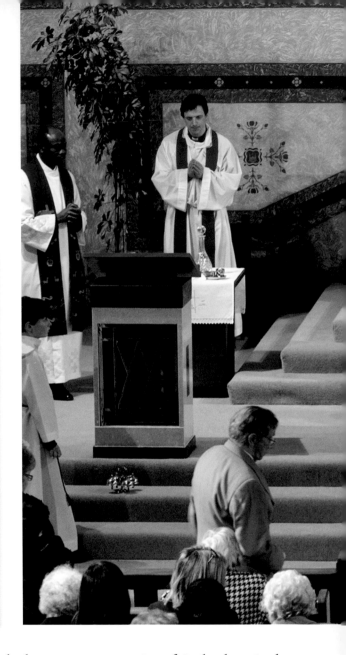

Catholic congregation receiving communion during a Mass celebrated by the Bishop of Salford Diocese in Manchester, England. The ritual of a Catholic Mass always remains the same, although the celebration may differ in terms of the building in which it is conducted, the music sung, and the language in which it is said.

Orthodox Numbers in the United States

Recent estimates indicate that there are around 6 million Orthodox in the United States. This includes members of the Orthodox Church of America, which is the name of the church that formerly was called the Russian Orthodox Greek Catholic Church of America. Other ethnic groups of Orthodox Christians (Albanians, Bulgarians, Romanians, Serbians, Syrians, and Ukrainians) arrived in the 20th century. Many of the Orthodox churches keep strong ties, at least in tradition and spirit, with their respective mother churches and train their clergy there.

bers in 1975, by far the largest representative of Orthodoxy in the Western world.

CATHOLIC DIVERSITY AND UNITY

The Catholic Church in America is a "melting pot" like America itself. Its members are not all descendants of western European countries. They also come from Africa, Asia, Australia, and South and Central America. Others (for example, Eastern Rite Catho-

lics), in smaller numbers, come from eastern Europe. They bring all their own varied traditions. Yet the hierarchical structure of the Catholic Church, while allowing room for diversity, tends to produce a strong unity of belief and practice.

Religious celebrations may vary in terms of the types of music, such as Gregorian chant in a Catholic monastery or guitar-led hymns in a university chapel, but the ritual of a Catholic Mass remains essentially fixed throughout the Catholic world. When

American Catholics travel to Saint Mark's Basilica in Venice or Saint Vitus's Cathedral in Prague, despite the language differences, they feel at home: The basic structure of the Mass is familiar. With the central authority of the pope and bishops and with required church approval of religious teachings and practices, the Catholic Church tends to preserve a bond of unified faith among its members throughout the world.

ORTHODOX DIVERSITY AND UNITY

The general tendency in Orthodox churches is toward independence. The early churches, prior to the rise of Rome's claim to be the head Church, always insisted on independent jurisdictions. This independent spirit has tended to show itself in the more national identity of the various Orthodox churches (Russian, Greek, Albanian, Bulgarian, Romanian, Serbian, etc.). The agreement in basic Christian doctrines and the uniform structure of the Divine Liturgy—daily services said in the Church—binds these churches to a common tradition of faith. Their diversity is often due to the influence of each church's ministry by its particular heritage.

THE MEANING OF *ORTHODOX*

In the ancient historical context the term *orthodox* described the teachings of all the churches that held to agreed teachings concerning the doctrine of the Trinity and the identity of Jesus Christ as one person who is both God and man. The teachings of both Rome and the churches of the East that were not deemed heretical were thus called *orthodox*. At first, then, it was a term applied to Western and Eastern churches that agreed with the teachings of the early ecumenical, or general, councils of the church. Only later did the term *orthodox* come to be attached to the churches that remained independent and not affiliated with Rome.

Catholic and Orthodox

The word *catholic* comes from the Greek word meaning "universal." "Go, teach all nations" was the command that Jesus Christ gave to his apostles. The word *orthodox* comes from the Greek *orthos,* meaning "right" or "correct," and *doxa,* meaning "belief" or "teaching."

Greek Orthodox monasteries built high on sandstone rock peaks at Meteora in Thessaly, Greece. Serving as communities for Orthodox monks who withdrew from the world to dedicate themselves to a life of study and prayer, 24 of these monasteries were built from the 11th century onward.

The Church of Saint George in Lalibela, in the Amhara region of Ethiopia. This rock-hewn church, built in the 13th century, is an important pilgrimage site for members of the Ethiopian Orthodox Church.

THE CHRISTIAN VIEW OF "OLD LAW, NEW LAW"

From the perspective of Catholic and Orthodox Christians, God's chosen people before Jesus Christ were a particular people, the Jewish people.

According to God's plan, revealed in the Old Testament scriptures, the Jews were, by their dedication to God's law and by their religious example, meant to influence other peoples and lead them to God. According to the Jewish law and the prophets, even as God's special people, they were meant by God to spread the message of divine care or concern for all peoples of the world to their neighbors. However, over time and because of persecution, conquest, and oppression, much of Judaism became more inward-looking and legalistic. Jesus Christ, by his interpretation of the Old Law and presentation of the New Law, released his followers from many of these specifically Jewish laws that set Jews apart. In the Catholic and Orthodox view he took the spirit of the Jewish law and gave it an interpretation that made it more universal.

Jesus Christ extended the law of love to a world beyond the Jewish people. It is this universal spiritual law that one of his disciples, Saint Paul, carried to the world outside of Palestine—to the people to whom he writes in his Epistles, or Letters. These people include the Galatians, the Ephesians, the Colossians, the Corinthians, and the Romans.

The spreading of Christ's teachings beyond these cities to the whole world has taken many centuries. In the Far East and in Muslim territories, its influence is still very small. Of the roughly 6.5 billion people in the world today, however, approximately 1.1 billion are Catholics and about 220 million more are Orthodox Christians.

A Universal Law

The Old Law of the Jewish tradition was reinterpreted by Christ to create a new universal law. It is best summed up in the following quote from Luke 10:25-28:

There was a lawyer who to disconcert him stood up and said to him, "Master, what must I do to inherit eternal life?" He said to him, "What is written in the Law? What do you read there?" He replied, "You must love the Lord your God with all your heart, with all your soul, with all your strength, and with all your mind, and your neighbor as yourself."
"You have answered right," said Jesus.
"Do this and life is yours."

PREACHING THE GOSPEL TO ALL NATIONS

The universal extension of the Catholic Church may be seen in the large crowds that have gathered for the late Pope John Paul II's many trips to South America, Africa, Asia, the Near East, and eastern Europe. Huge crowds have also gathered for the journeys of the present pope, Benedict XV1, in Europe, Brazil, the United States, and Australia. It can be noticed in the large percentage of Catholics throughout the world, for example, Mexico (94 percent), Argentina (91 percent), the Philippines (88 percent), Italy (97 percent), Poland (92 percent), and the United States (21 percent). On a grander scale, the universal drive of the Catholic Church can be discovered in the growing numbers of Catholics in Africa.

Although the Catholic Church is viewed by most people as a Western church anchored in Rome, this does not give a completely accurate or representative picture. There are also Eastern Rite Catholic Churches that once were not part of the Roman Church but that, over centuries, have entered into union with Rome. Thus, in the United States and abroad, Romanian Catholics, Ukrainian Catholics, Armenian Catholics, Melkite Catholics, and many other forms of Eastern Catholics, are united in faith with the large number of Catholics of Western background.

The international spread of the Orthodox Church can be seen not just in its heartlands of Russia, eastern Europe, Greece, the Middle East and North Africa, but in its many churches in the United Kingdom, United States, Latin America, and even China. While often restricted by its strong ethnic links, which make each Church ethno-centric, modern patriarchs such as the Ecumenical Patriarch Bartolomeuw have travelled extensively linking churches and communities and

ORTHODOX NUMBERS WORLDWIDE

Of the world's approximately 220 million Orthodox Christians, the largest numbers are found in the Greek and Russian Orthodox churches. Three-quarters of the world's Orthodox Christians are Europeans. The next largest group, about 17 percent, is found in Africa. Asia, especially the Near East, has about 6 percent of the Orthodox population. The United States and Canada now claim about 6.6 million Orthodox Christians, more than 3 percent of the world population, whereas South America numbers a little over 500,000 members. Orthodox missionaries are also now active around the world.

working with other Christian traditions such as Catholicism and the major Protestant churches.

THE CHURCH'S MISSION

Christ gave his church a mission to seek the return of all humanity and all aspects of human life to his father in heaven. For all Christians, Christ continues to live in the church and its mem-

American Catholic Relief Services distributing food aid at a center in Mongu, Zambia. The Catholic Relief Services, the official international relief and development agency of the Catholic community in the United States, assists people in 98 countries on the basis of need, not race, creed, or nationality. The Catholic Relief Services creates opportunities for Catholics in the United States to live their faith by providing financial support and addressing the root causes of poverty.

bers, and through him the church has the power and guidance to teach and to promote the spiritual life of his followers.

Every aspect of a Christian's life is linked to Christ. Christians attempt to imitate the devotion Christ had to always follow his father's will. Saint Paul often speaks of the members of the church as the body of Christ and of Christ himself as the head of the church. The church gets its universality from its head, Jesus Christ, and its mission is to bring Christ's helping grace to all creation. That is why its members are called to redeem all things. In their attempts to accomplish this mission, they are called to help people in need and to comfort, forgive, and bear wrongs patiently.

BRINGING THE TEACHINGS OF CHRIST

It is not unusual to visit a sick friend or relative at a hospital with a name like Saint Clare's or Saint Jude's. Neither is it unexpected that lodging for the homeless will be found in hospices supported by Catholic and Orthodox churches. Nor is it surprising to see the Eucharist from a Catholic Mass or an Orthodox Divine Liturgy being brought to the homebound sick. These are the ordinary actions that show Christians' efforts to bring the compassion of Christ to all.

LIVING THE CHRISTIAN MESSAGE

There are also the extraordinary efforts of dedicated Christians around the world. The followers of the late Mother Teresa (1910–97) are famous in all nations for their dedication to the poor and the sick of Kolkata (Calcutta) and many other cities. Today, especially in Europe, there are

The "Works of Mercy"

The "works of mercy," both physical and spiritual—giving help and comfort to those in need, offering forgiveness and tolerance—are embodiments of the words spoken by Christ himself in chapter 25 of Matthew's Gospel:

Come, you that are blessed by my Father, inherit the kingdom prepared for you from the foundation of the world: for I was hungry and you gave me food, I was thirsty and you gave me something to drink, I was a stranger and you welcomed me, I was naked and you gave me clothing. I was sick and you took care of me, I was in prison and you visited me. Then the righteous will answer him, "Lord, when was it that we saw you hungry and gave you food, or thirsty and gave you something to drink?" . . . And the king will answer them, "Truly I tell you, just as you did it to one of the least of these who are members of my family, you did it to me."

—Matthew 25:34–40

many Roman Catholic lay communities that combine an ordinary life in the world with regular communal prayer and service to the poor. In the Middle East Father Elias Chacour (1939–), an Arab Eastern Catholic priest, is known for his efforts to bring about nonviolent cooperation and understanding between Palestinians and Israelis. In Russia the Russian Orthodox martyr Father Alexander Men (1935–90) was a popular priest known for his holiness and dynamic preaching. He proclaimed the Christian message boldly even while under constant KGB, or Secret Police, surveillance and intimidation. He was struck by an ax and killed on September 9, 1990.

MISSION WORK

In almost every city and town in America ordinary examples of the works of mercy are visible today. They have become traditional. Many of the missions American Catholics and Orthodox assign to churches and church institutions are part of what they inherited from eastern and western Europe, Africa, South America, and Canada. Their many welcoming practices and festive celebrations were and are ways of feeding the hungry, clothing the naked, and welcoming the strangers from foreign lands.

When Germans and Italians arrived in America in the late 19th and early 20th centuries, they discovered Catholic churches founded by their predecessors that made them feel at home. Celebrations of the Feast of Saint Anthony in the North End of Boston, on Mott Street in New York City, and on the streets of Cassino, Italy, have remarkable similarities that bring warmth and comfort to the hearts of Italian Catholics.

The blessing of the Portuguese fishing fleet would be as familiar to the people of Gloucester, Massachusetts, and Newport Beach, California, as to those of Lisbon or Oporto in Portugal. The Portuguese celebration of the Feast of the Blessed Sacrament in August 2005 drew more than 300,000 visitors to New Bedford, Massachusetts.

French Canadians who poured into New England in the latter part of the 19th century brought with them their language

The Catholic Mission Basilica of San Diego de Alcala was the first Christian church in California. It was founded on July 16, 1769, by Blessed Junipero Serra. It was the first of a series of mission churches in California established by Spanish missionaries and settlers.

and celebrations. A New England Catholic of French Canadian background would feel quite at home at the Church of Notre Dame in Montreal, at the shrine of Saint Anne de Beaupré just outside Quebec, or in a small town church in the rural villages of northern Maine or Vermont.

Many Orthodox and Eastern Catholic churches hold annual national conferences in different regions of the United States to teach their faithful their spiritual traditions, to celebrate the Divine Liturgy, and to cherish their ethnic heritage.

WELCOMING NEW ARRIVALS

In the name of Christ, Catholics and Orthodox Christians in these ordinary situations made their fellow countrymen feel at home. Many of these welcoming practices survive today and have been extended to new arrivals from the Spanish-speaking countries of Central and South America, to Catholic immigrants from Southeast Asia, and to the Catholics and Orthodox from eastern Europe and the Near East.

When Jesus told his followers to "go and make disciples of all nations," he added the words: "and remember, I am with you always, to the end of the age" (Matthew 28:19–20). Catholics and Orthodox believe that Christ acts through them as his instruments. As creatures of a loving God they have their God-given natural abilities. As instruments of Christ's mission to bring salvation to the whole world, they believe that Christ acts through them when they feed the hungry, comfort the troubled, visit the bed-ridden, welcome a stranger, or heal the sick.

THE COMMITMENT TO EDUCATION

Realizing that the American public schools could not foster any particular religious beliefs, Catholics and Orthodox decided to build their own schools. As necessity demanded they built elementary schools, high schools, colleges, and universities. This strong commitment to education is not new.

NOURISHING AND STRENGTHENING FAITH

The early Christian writers of the East and West realized the importance of education. Saints Basil and Gregory of Nyssa from the East and Saints Jerome and Augustine from the West argued that Christians could defend themselves against opponents only if they were good at rhetoric, and that they could explain their faith coherently and intelligently only if they were adept at logic. Saint Augustine in the fifth century particularly urged Christians to pursue any studies "by which our most wholesome faith, which leads to eternal life, may be begotten, nourished, strengthened, and defended" (*On the Trinity*, XIV, 1).

CATHOLIC EDUCATION

In the 16th, 17th, and 18th centuries in Italy and France, a large number of Catholic religious communities of women were formed that were dedicated to education. They have continued to carry out their work of educating the young throughout Europe as well as in the many primary and secondary religious schools they founded in the United States and Canada.

ORTHODOX EDUCATION

The Orthodox tradition of education goes back to its earliest days and has always been central and fundamental to the building of a Christian community. This is especially the case with the Greek Orthodox who have established, for example, Hellenic College and the Holy Cross Greek Orthodox Theological School in Boston, Massachusetts. Saint Vladimir's Seminary in West-wood, New York, under the auspices of the Orthodox Church of America, is one of the most prestigious seminaries in the world. These institutions continue a long educational tradition of the Orthodox churches.

THE SPIRITUAL WAY OF LIFE AND WORSHIP

For Catholics, as well as for Orthodox Christians, all these works of mercy that show Christ's enduring presence in today's world have merit only if they are performed in union with Christ. This common vision of the role of Christ in Catholic and Orthodox life is well expressed in *The Catechism of the Catholic Church*.

Christ is always present in his Church, especially in her liturgical celebrations. He is present in the Sacrifice of the Mass [or Divine Liturgy] not only in the person of his minister, "the same now offering, through the minis-try of priests, who formerly offered himself on the cross," but especially in the Eucharistic species. By his power he is present in the sacraments so that when anybody baptizes, it is really Christ himself who baptizes. He is present in his word since it is he himself who speaks when the holy Scriptures are read in the Church. Lastly, he is present when the Church prays and sings, for he has promised "where two or three are gathered together in my name there am I in the midst of them." (1088)

Catholics and Orthodox Christians believe that the ideas expressed in this declaration hold not only for official religious celebrations but for all good works. It is Christ who works through believers as they reach out to their neighbors. He teaches when they teach. He forgives when they forgive. He heals when they care for the sick. He reaches out when they extend a helping hand. He blesses when they embrace the suffering and the oppressed.

CHAPTER 2

THE ORIGINS OF THE CATHOLIC AND ORTHODOX CHURCHES

Christians speak of the Jewish people's religious history as told in the Holy Books—the Hebrew Bible—as the Old Testament. They describe the Ten Commandments, and all the laws found in the Jewish scriptures, as the Old Law. They refer to the agreement between God and his chosen people—a pact whereby God would watch over the Jews in a special way and they, for their part, would obey his commandments—as the Old Covenant. In contrast, in speaking of their own religious association with God, Catholics and Orthodox Christians, like all Christians, speak of the New Testament, the New Law, and the New Covenant.

CONTINUITY AND DISCONTINUITY

Since the church is the community that continues the covenant God made with his chosen people, many of the images of the Old Covenant or Old Testament carry over into the New Covenant or

A congregation in front of the altar of the Catholic Church of San Jeronimo el Real in Madrid, Spain. The Church was originally founded in 1464 and reconstructed in its present setting in 1503 for Ferdinand and Isabel, king of Aragon and queen of Castile.

Stained-glass window depicting Moses receiving the tablets of the Law upon which the Ten Commandments were written.

Testament. The church continues to be the community of God's people, those whom he chose to make his special people. One of the descriptions of the church, then, is "the people of God." "People of God" is an image taken from the Old Testament. It is an image that is worth examining to appreciate the new meaning that was given to it in the New Testament. It is an image that begins with the story of Abraham.

ABRAHAM AND THE COVENANT WITH GOD

In the opening book of the Bible, Genesis, Abraham is introduced. It is with him especially that the story of God's covenant with humanity begins:

I will make you exceedingly fruitful; and I will make nations of you, and kings shall come from you. I will establish my covenant between me and you, and your offspring after you throughout their generations, for an everlasting covenant, to be God to you and to your offspring after you. And I will give to you, and to your offspring after you, the land where you are now an alien, all the land of Canaan, for a perpetual holding; and I will be their God. —Genesis 17:6–8

God thereby made a covenant with Abraham and his offspring. They would be his special people and he would be their God. For Catholics and Orthodox Christians, this covenant with Abraham tells them something about their own New Covenant with God. They would be God's new special people and he would be their God. Their new inheritance as children of God did not totally negate the Old Covenant. For example, the famous Ten Commandments given to Moses by God as rules to live by are central to Christian understanding of proper moral behavior and have helped shape law throughout the Christian world.

THE COMING MESSIAH

The frequent domination of the Jewish people by more powerful nations inspired hope for a new leader who might free them from their oppressors. In the years before Jesus Christ's birth prophets

THE TEN COMMANDMENTS

I am the Lord your God, who brought you out of the land of Egypt, out of the house of slavery; you shall have no other gods before me.

You shall not make for yourself an idol, whether in the form of anything that is in heaven above, or that is on the earth beneath, or that is in the water under the earth. You shall not bow down to them or worship them; for I the Lord your God am a jealous God, punishing children for iniquity of parents, to the third and fourth generation of those who reject me, but showing steadfast love to the thousandth generation of those who love me and keep my commandments.

You shall not make wrongful use of the name of the Lord your God, for the Lord will not acquit anyone who misuses his name.

Remember the Sabbath day, and keep it holy . . .

Honor your father and your mother, so that your days may be long in the land that the Lord your God is giving you.

You shall not murder.

You shall not commit adultery.

You shall not steal.

You shall not bear false witness against your neighbor.

You shall not covet your neighbor's house; you shall not covet your neighbor's wife, or male or female slave, or ox, or donkey, or anything that belongs to your neighbor.

—Exodus 20:2–17

foretold the coming of a Messiah who would save God's people and establish the kingdom promised to Abraham. This Messiah was pictured in different ways by Jewish writers: some imagined him as a military leader overthrowing their oppressors; others expected him to be a great teacher; still others, more rarely, thought of him as a suffering servant.

EXPECTATIONS FOR A MESSIAH

Matthew's Gospel introduces Jesus Christ with the following words: "An account of the genealogy of Jesus the Messiah, the son of David, the son of Abraham" (Matthew 1:1). Jesus is thus presented as the offspring of Abraham, from whom a great nation would descend. He is also, like David, a king who can lead his people.

The opening words of this Gospel, then, recall the long-held hopes of the Jewish people who had been oppressed for so many centuries. It was during these days of high expectations for a Messiah that Jesus began to preach among the Jewish people.

Some saw this wandering preacher as merely another rabbi, or teacher, who spent his days interpreting and reshaping Jewish Law. Others saw him as a leader in their fight against Roman rule. Still others saw him as the Messiah, sent by God to deliver them.

THE FOUR EVANGELISTS

The principal source of information about his life is the New Testament of the Christian Bible, especially the Gospels of Matthew, Mark, Luke, and John. Stories about the life and deeds of Jesus Christ and what

BOOKS OF THE NEW TESTAMENT

Gospels—Matthew, Mark, Luke, John
Acts of the Apostles
Letters:
Romans
1 Corinthians
2 Corinthians
Galatians
Ephesians
Philippians
Colossians
1 Thessalonians
2 Thessalonians
1 Timothy
2 Timothy
Titus
Philemon
Hebrews
James
1 Peter
2 Peter
1 John
2 John
3 John
Jude
Revelation

he taught circulated first by word of mouth. Later they were collected and written down. It was from such oral and written sources that the Gospels of the four evangelists were compiled. The first of these, the Gospel of Mark, was written about 62 C.E., only 30 years after the death of Jesus. Written so soon after the events they describe, these books present a strong body of evidence for the existence of Jesus and the content of his preaching.

THE GOSPEL ACCOUNT OF JESUS' YOUTH

The Gospels tell little about the childhood of Jesus. Following the customs of the time he most likely began to work alongside his earthly father, Joseph, learning the trade of carpenter. He would have followed the ritual observances of the Jewish law and studied the Old Testament stories. Luke's Gospel tells us that when Jesus was 12 years old he went with his mother Mary and with Joseph to Jerusalem to celebrate the Passover at the Temple—the heart of Judaism and its rituals. Unknown to Mary and Joseph, Jesus stayed behind as the caravan headed back to Nazareth. When they discovered that he was missing, they went back to Jerusalem to find him. "They found him in the Temple, sitting among the teachers, listening to them and asking them questions." (Luke 2:46)

When Jesus was about 30 years old a preacher called John the Baptist began a new religious movement. He announced to the people the coming of the Messiah ("the Anointed One") and urged them to prepare for his arrival by repenting of their sins. John used flowing water as a sign of washing away their sins. As he preached John baptized people by immersing them in the water of the River Jordan. Jesus was one of the many who went to John to be baptized.

Jesus began his own ministry, preaching repentance and telling his listeners "to believe in the good news": that the kingdom of God or the kingdom of heaven is near. The "gospel," or the "good news," that Jesus taught in his sermons and stories was new. Yet he insisted that he was not setting aside the Old Law but was extending and enriching it.

A stained-glass window depicting John the Baptist. According to the Gospel of Mark (1:7–8) Jesus approached John to be baptized and John proclaimed: "The one who is more powerful than I is coming after me; I am not worthy to stoop down and untie the thong of his sandals. I have baptized you with water; but he will baptize you with the Holy Spirit."

JESUS AS THE NEW LAWGIVER

In Chapter 5 of his Gospel Matthew tells about Jesus' Sermon on the Mount. This sermon sets up many parallels with Moses' reception of the Ten Commandments of the Old Law. First of all, like Moses' reception of the Ten Commandments, it takes place on a mountain. Next it sets a deliberately different tone from the "Thou shalt nots" of the Old Testament code:

Blessed are the poor in spirit, for theirs is the kingdom of heaven. Blessed are those who mourn, for they shall be comforted. Blessed are the meek, for they shall inherit the earth. Blessed are those who hunger and thirst for righteousness, for they shall be satisfied. Blessed are the merciful, for they shall obtain mercy. Blessed are the pure in heart, for they shall see God. Blessed are the peacemakers, for they shall be called sons of God. Blessed are those who are persecuted for righteousness' sake, for theirs is the kingdom of heaven. —Matthew 5:3–10

The scribes and Pharisees, experts in the interpretation of the Old Testament Law, challenged Jesus' teachings concerning the New Law and his interpretation of the texts of the Old Law. On many occasions they tried to entrap Jesus with their questions. Jesus, however, defended himself and justified his interpretation of the Old Law.

JESUS AS SUFFERING SERVANT

Jesus' preaching had made him well known. When he traveled from Galilee to Jerusalem for Passover his entry into the city was triumphal. According to Matthew's Gospel (21:8–11) crowds of

THE TWELVE APOSTLES OF CHRIST

The four Gospels give varying names of the Twelve Apostles. According to the Gospels of Mark and Matthew, the Twelve Apostles, or disciples, were chosen by Jesus near the beginning of his ministry. Jesus described the role he offered the apostles as the "fishers of men" because most of the original disciples were actual fishermen from the Sea of Galilee. Jesus taught and trained his disciples and after his death and resurrection, it was the apostles who spread the teachings of Jesus.

Peter
Andrew
James, the son of Zebedee
John
Philip
Bartholomew
Thomas
Matthew, the tax collector
James, the son of Alphaeus
Thaddaeus
Simon, the Cananean
Judas Iscariot

—Matthew 6:9–13

people were proclaiming him the Messiah. In the traditional Eastern manner, many honored him by throwing their cloaks in front of him, and others cut branches from trees and spread them in his path.

However, when Jesus' presence in Jerusalem became known to the priests of the Temple and to the Pharisees and scribes, these teachers and lawyers began to plot against him. These religious leaders attacked Jesus for his disregard of the legal and ceremonial aspects of Jewish laws and for his preaching of spiritual and moral reform.

When Jesus arrived at the Temple he assailed the irreverence that he found there. Instead of a holy place, he found it to be a noisy bazaar, or market. People were selling doves and animals to be offered as sacrifices and shouting out the rates of money exchange. Jesus overturned the tables of the money-changers and the seats of those who sold doves and said to them: "It is written, 'My house shall be called a house of prayer,' but you are making it a den of robbers." (Matthew 21:13) The chief priests and scribes challenged him, asking, "By what authority are you doing these things, and who gave you this authority?" (Matthew 21:23) Jesus sensed the danger such questions implied and the growing anger of the scribes, the Pharisees, and the chief priests against him.

THE LAST SUPPER

For Passover, a major feast celebrating the release of the Jews from Egyptian slavery, Jesus and his 12 disciples gathered in the house of one of his followers to have supper together.

During this Passover meal Jesus spoke the words that are the foundation for the Catholic and Orthodox sacrament of the

Eucharist. "While they were eating, Jesus took a loaf of bread, and after blessing it he broke it, gave it to the disciples, and said, 'Take, eat; this is my body.' Then he took a cup, and after giving thanks he gave it to them, saying, 'Drink from it, all of you, for this is my blood of the covenant, which is poured out for many for the forgiveness of sins." (Matthew 26:26–28) It was also during the Passover meal that Jesus revealed that he would be betrayed by one of his disciples.

Wall painting of the Last Supper. It was during this meal that Jesus taught his disciples an important lesson. Jesus washed his disciples' feet, saying to them, "Now I have set you an example, that you should do as I have done. Very truly I tell you, servants are not greater than their master; nor are messengers greater than the one who sent them."
—John 13:15–16

The Betrayal

During the Passover meal Jesus revealed that he would be betrayed by one of his disciples: "Truly, I tell you, one of you will betray me." (Matthew 26:21) Judas left the room. Jesus' departing words as they left the supper were:

Little children, I am with you only a little longer. You will look for me; and as I said to the Jews so now I say to you, "Where I am going, you cannot come." I give you a new commandment, that you love one another. Just as I have loved you, you also should love one another. By this everyone will know that you are my disciples, if you have love for one another.

—John 13:33–35

A Russian icon of Jesus being taken down from the cross by his followers. The Gospels report the main witnesses at the Crucifixion: "Many women were also there, looking on from a distance; they had followed Jesus from Galilee and had provided for him. Among them were Mary Magdalene, and Mary the mother of James and Joseph, and the mother of the sons of Zebedee." —Matthew 27:55–56, Mark 15:40–41, Luke 23:49

JESUS' CRUCIFIXION AND DEATH

The Gospels tell of Jesus' last days. After the Last Supper, Jesus went to a garden called Gethsemane at the foot of the Mount of Olives in Jerusalem, where he often went for prayer. On that night the disciples went with him. As his disciples slept around him the prayerful silence of the garden was broken by the arrival of Judas, leading a band of soldiers.

Jesus was arrested and brought before the Sanhedrin, or council of religious leaders. They found Jesus guilty of calling himself the Son of God. However, Roman law prevented them from putting him to death on the basis of their own laws. To ensure his death they brought him before Pontius Pilate, the Roman official, and charged him not only with blasphemy but also with organizing a revolt against Rome. Despite his hesitancy Pilate gave in to the religious leaders and sentenced Jesus to death by crucifixion.

Pontius Pilate ordered a sign nailed to Jesus' cross to mock him and the claim that was made that he was the King of the Jews. "Jesus of Nazareth, King of the Jews," it said in Aramaic, Greek, and Latin. (John 19:19–20) That is why many crosses today carry the initials "INRI," which is the abbreviation for the Latin version of this phrase.

As the soldiers and the mob taunted the dying Jesus, he prayed: "Father, forgive them, for they know not what they do." (Luke 23:34) Finally, after hours of unbearable pain, he cried out, "My God, my God, why hast thou forsaken me?" (Matthew 27:46) Then he died. A Roman officer reported to Pilate that Jesus was dead. Christ's body was turned over to one of his followers, Joseph of Arimathea,

"By his bruises we are healed"

Crucifixion was the form of death reserved by the Romans for thieves and revolutionaries. Matthew, however, in his Gospel (Matthew 8:17), sees Jesus' sufferings as the fulfillment of Isaiah's prophecy that the Messiah would be a suffering servant:

He was despised and rejected by others; a man of suffering and acquainted with infirmity; and as one from whom others hide their faces he was despised, and we held him of no account. Surely he has borne our infirmities and carried our diseases; yet we accounted him stricken, struck down by God, and afflicted. But he was wounded for our transgressions, crushed for our iniquities; upon him was the punishment that made us whole, and by his bruises we are healed.

—Isaiah 53:3–5

for burial. It was wrapped in a linen shroud and placed in a tomb that was sealed with a large rock.

THE RESURRECTION OF JESUS

According to Matthew's Gospel, on the third day after Jesus was crucified Mary Magdalene and Mary, the mother of James and Joseph, went to see the sepulchre, the tomb in a cave where Jesus was buried. However Jesus was not there. An angel had descended from heaven and rolled back the stone. He told the women: "Do

Detail from a tapestry in the Vatican in Rome showing the resurrected Christ against the background of the tomb in which he was buried.

not be afraid; I know that you are looking for Jesus who was crucified. . . . He has been raised from the dead." (Matthew 28:2–6) Later, according to the Gospel, Christ appeared to the 11 disciples and commissioned them to preach the gospel and baptize:

All authority in heaven and on earth has been given to me. Go therefore and make disciples of all nations, baptizing them in the name of the Father, and of the Son, and of the Holy Spirit, teaching them to observe all that I have commanded you; and lo, I am with you always to the close of the age.
—Matthew 28:18–20

It is with this commission and promise that the church began and continues to this day to bear witness to the living Christ who has overcome death.

THE CHRISTIAN VIEW OF BIBLICAL HISTORY

For Catholics and Orthodox Christians, the biblical stories are not just recollections of historical happenings. They manifest God's involvement with his chosen people and the lessons he wanted to teach them by the various events of his providential care. To understand Christ and his church it is necessary to appreciate as well as possible God's whole involvement with humankind. Events in biblical history shed light on God's plan for all of creation.

Images and stories from the Old Testament reappear remolded in the New Testament. For example the story of Abraham tells something about Christ. Moses' commandments tell something about the Sermon on the Mount. The Jews' escape from the slavery of Egypt tells something about the escape of all from the slavery of sin. The sacrifice of a lamb in the Jerusalem Temple tells about the sacrifice of Christ, the Lamb of God, on the cross. Each part of the biblical story tells something about the other parts. This is why the story of the origin of the church needs the whole of the Old and New Testaments to show how the church fits into the whole of God's plan for humanity's redemption and the role of the church in it.

CHAPTER 3

THE HISTORY OF THE CATHOLIC AND ORTHODOX CHURCHES

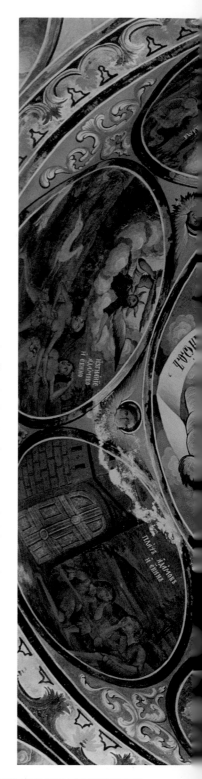

According to Catholic and Orthodox belief, it was 40 days after Jesus Christ's resurrection from the dead that he ascended into heaven. According to the Acts of the Apostles, Christ's ascension left his disciples lonely and confused. They no longer had a teacher to follow, and they were afraid that they too would be punished. As they huddled together in fear and bewilderment, the Acts of the Apostles reports that:

Suddenly from heaven there came a sound like a violent wind, and it filled the entire house where they were sitting. Divided tongues, as of fire, appeared among them, and a tongue rested on each of them. All of them were filled with the Holy Spirit and began to speak in other languages, as the Spirit gave them ability.
—Acts 2:2–4

The painted ceiling of a Bulgarian church. At the center is God the Father; the surrounding scenes depict the story of Adam and Eve in the Garden of Eden from the book of Genesis in the Old Testament of the Bible.

After being filled with the Holy Spirit, according to the Christian scriptures, the apostles gained courage and became missionaries, fulfilling the final directive of their risen and ascended Lord: "Go therefore and make disciples of all nations, baptizing them in the name of the Father and of the Son and of the Holy Spirit." (Matthew 28:19) They went about teaching the main Christian message: that Jesus was the true son promised to Abraham, that he was the Messiah, that he was the Son of God who became man, that he was crucified and raised from the dead, and that through him sins are forgiven and eternal salvation is offered to all people.

THE EARLY CHRISTIAN CHURCH

The first Christians were the disciples of Christ, the simple fishermen who followed him. The first Christian "church" was the Jewish community that had heard Jesus preach, watched the wonders he performed, and saw in him a great prophet and then more than a prophet.

The early origins of the Christian church are hardly distinguishable from a special Jewish community. Many Jews saw Christ as a special rabbi, a special teacher. Only gradually did they come to believe that Christ was more than just a teacher and that he had a larger mission. At first they continued to perform all the Jewish rituals on the Sabbath. Little by little they reenacted the Passover meal with its new meaning, realizing that Christ had, by his death and resurrection, given it a new reality. As the fuller meaning of Christ's life and teaching dawned on them, Christian historians tell us, they began to separate from the Temple and synagogue. It is this stage of development that is chronicled in the Gospel of Matthew, at times called "the Gospel of the Jewish Christian community."

NEW MEANINGS AND A NEW VISION

Christians believe that Christ was a teacher, but also one who gave a New Law in his own name, thereby indicating that he was God. When he spoke of God as his father, he spoke, according to

Christian believers, as one equal to his father. They believe that his teachings gave a whole new meaning to the Old Law, and his death was a sacrifice that replaced all the sacrifices of the Old Law. His resurrection, according to Christian faith, was a guarantee of his claims and of his promises. These claims also called for believers to have the same kind of faith in God as Abraham had. Christ called not just for obedience to a Law; he called for a new faith that believed the new meanings and the new vision he brought to human life. These themes of the Jewish community of Christians, sounded in Matthew's Gospel, also are the themes of the Epistle to the Hebrews. Both these writings put us in touch with the first community of Christians—the Jewish community of Christians.

THE GOSPEL PREACHED TO THE GENTILES

Paul, a key writer of the New Testament who was martyred in 64, may have preached to the Jews (also known sometimes as Hebrews), but it is not for that work that he is best known. As he says in his Letter to the Galatians, a Gentile (non-Jewish) people to whom he had preached about Christ, he had been a very fervent Jew. He studied under the great Rabbi Gamaliel. He even persecuted the Christians and was present at the death of the first Christian martyr, Stephen. However, God brought him to a dramatic conversion. His original name was Saul of the city of Tarsus, but after his conversion he used the Greek version of his name, Paul, and it is as Paul that he is known as the Apostle to the Gentiles.

Paul's letters to the many Christian communities show a man of tireless energy and daring adventures. His journeys are recounted in the Acts of the Apostles, Chapters 13–28.

There were tensions in these very early days of the church. Some favored a more Jewish form of Christianity. Paul argued that this was "another Gospel," that is, a distorted Gospel, and that the New Law as preached by Jesus Christ should be followed.

After much dispute with those who wanted to preserve the Christian ties with the Jewish tradition, Paul's argument won out.

The church would be built on the foundation of the New Law as taught by Christ himself.

DISSENSION AND PERSECUTION

Christian historians report that late in his life and ministry, the chief apostle Peter made his way to Rome, the capital city of the Roman Empire, preaching the apostolic faith and establishing a Christian community. Paul, a convert from Judaism, also traveled through the Gentile world; he too, after "journeying often," arrived in Rome. It was there that both Peter and Paul met their deaths, probably in the same year (64 C.E.), at the orders of the emperor Nero (37–68 C.E.).

A procession leaving a monastery on Mount Athos following the celebration of the Divine Liturgy. Mount Athos is situated on the eastern peninsula of Halkidiki in Greece. It is called the Holy Mount and covers 218 square miles (350 square kilometers). The entire eastern peninsula is given to Orthodox monasteries and hermitages. Land is managed by the monks who live there. As a self-governing part of the Greek state, it is divided into 21 territories, each with a cardinal monastery and a series of monastic establishments surrounding it.

Carving of a fish on the wall of a cave used as a chapel by the 7th-century Saint Fillan in Pittenweem (meaning "place of the cave") in Fife, Scotland. This is one of the most significant sites of the early Christian church in Scotland. The fish became a symbol of Christ for early Christians, since the Greek word for fish was *icthus,* which was an abbreviation for *Iesus Christos theou uios soter* (Jesus Christ, the Son of God, Savior).

SOWING THE SEEDS OF FAITH

This was the beginning of 300 years of persecution for the Christians by the Roman authorities. Most of the persecution was local and intermittent. Occasionally it extended to a general persecution of all the Christians in the empire. Such a persecution occurred under the emperor Decius (201–251) in 250. Decius demanded that all citizens of the empire sacrifice to the Roman gods. Those Christians who refused to do so were imprisoned, tortured, or killed. Many Christians died for their faith. Their martyrdom sowed the seeds of faith in the hearts of many converts. For those persecuted after the manner of Christ, it turned an era of suffering and bloodshed into an age of promise for a harvest of new believers.

INTERPRETING THE GOSPEL

As Christianity grew, its troubles and growing pains came not only from the external source of the Roman authorities but also from its own ranks. Many Christians struggled to interpret the meaning of the Gospel and its lessons. From the beginning Christianity was not limited to the performance of certain rituals, nor even to a certain code of moral behavior. Rather, it proclaimed a new message that touched upon the whole of reality in all of its depth and breadth. The proper interpretation of this message

The writers of the early Christian church who explained and defended the orthodox teaching were later called the fathers of the church. They earned this title because they were considered to be the begetters of spiritual children who held to the true faith. The earliest were Ignatius of Antioch (30–107), Clement of Rome (30–100), Justin Martyr (ca. 100–ca. 165), and Irenaeus (120–202). They were later joined by Clement of Alexandria (ca. 150–ca. 215), Origen (ca. 185–254), Tertullian (ca. 160–ca. 225), and Cyprian (200–58).

of the Gospel was sometimes the subject of disagreement and debate. At various points in its history the Christian community has had to declare which interpretations were consistent with the essential message of the Gospel and which were not. Those that were not were called "heresies," meaning that they were misinterpretations of the message of the Gospel. The interpretations that were consistent with the essential message of the Gospel were declared "correct" or "orthodox."

THE GRADUAL ACCEPTANCE OF CHRISTIANITY

After many years of rejection and persecution Christians began to gain some acceptance. At first they were merely tolerated. However, by the time of Constantine (280–337), who is considered the first Christian emperor of Rome, they had achieved favored status. Around 380 Christianity became the accepted religion of the Roman Empire.

TENSIONS BETWEEN EASTERN AND WESTERN CHRISTIANITY

Not only had Constantine made Christianity the favored religion of the empire, he had also moved the empire's capital in 330 from Rome to Byzantium, a city in Ancient Greece, which he renamed Constantinople. This seat of political power then became a center of ecclesiastical importance. Rome retained a place of honor, but Constantinople, Antioch, Alexandria, and Jerusalem in the eastern half of the Roman Empire were regional centers that made claims of independence in the running of the regional churches under their care.

ECUMENICAL COUNCILS

General, or ecumenical councils were organized to discuss important matters of Christian belief. The participants included the regional and local bishops or their representatives from Rome, Constantinople, Antioch, Alexandria, and Jerusalem, along with their doctrinal advisers. The first such council was held in 325 at Nicea, where Arius, who raised questions about the nature of the divinity of Christ, was condemned as a heretic. Nicea, now called Iznik, is in modern day Turkey, and Arius was a theologian and priest who taught that Christ was not eternal but subordinate to God the Father. By claiming this, Arius was denying a core teaching of the church—that the three Persons of the Trinity were equal. The second ecumenical council, held in 381 at Constantinople, formulated a creed, or statement, of fundamental Christian beliefs. Called the Constantinopolitan/Nicene Creed, this statement is still recited in Catholic and Orthodox churches today.

FIRST DOCTRINAL BREAKS

The first doctrinal breaks in the unity of the Christian church occurred in the fifth century after debates concerning the divinity of Christ. The Council of Ephesus (431) condemned Nestorius, the archbishop of Constantinople, for teaching that there were two persons in Christ: the divine and the human. The church in what was then the Sassanid Empire (now Iraq and Iran) separated from the western churches of Rome and Constantinople after the Council of Ephesus. Today it is known as the Assyrian Church of the East. This "Church of the East" was immensely successful in its mission and by the seventh century had spread to China and Japan.

Similarly, in 451 the Council of Chalcedon condemned the Monophysites, a

CHRISTIAN BELIEFS

Probably the oldest and simplest creedal statement is the Apostles' Creed, developed in the first and second centuries and first recorded in 390.

I believe in God, the Father Almighty, creator of heaven and earth.

I believe in Jesus Christ, his only Son, our Lord.

He was conceived by the power of the Holy Spirit and born of the Virgin Mary.

He suffered under Pontius Pilate, was crucified, died and was buried.

He descended to the dead.

On the third day he rose again.

He ascended into heaven, and is seated at the right hand of the Father. He will come again to judge the living and the dead.

I believe in the Holy Spirit, the Holy Catholic Church, the communion of the Saints, the forgiveness of sins, and the resurrection of the body, and the life everlasting.

group that believed that there was only the divine nature in Christ. The "Monophysite" churches of Armenia, Syria, Egypt, Ethiopia, and India, known today as the Oriental Orthodox Churches, broke away from the Orthodox churches after the Council of Chalcedon.

EARLY PROBLEMS IN THE CHURCH

The Roman acceptance of Christianity gradually brought with it a number of problems. In the past being a Christian often came at personal risk, but it was becoming increasingly conventional, and even socially advantageous, to be a Christian. Thus there were a growing number of Christians who were Christian only in name and not very serious about their faith. Perhaps as a reaction to this phenomenon, some Christians began to search for ways to live out their faith in a more perfect manner.

THE MONASTIC MOVEMENT

One such way was the development of monasticism, a movement that began in Egypt in the fourth century and quickly spread throughout the Christian world. The monastic movement is the ancient source of the present-day religious orders in the Catholic Church and the communities of monks and nuns in the Orthodox and Eastern Catholic churches. The origins of the monastic movement are usually traced back to a man named Anthony (251–356), who lived in Egypt in the fourth century. Monastic life entailed a withdrawal from worldly affairs in favor of dedication to a religious life of poverty, chastity, and obedience.

THE FALL OF ROME

Another problem raised by Christianity's acceptance by the Roman world was that many non-Christians began to blame

A fresco of monks eating in Monte Oliveto Maggiore Catholic Abbey in Tuscany, Italy. Monastic communities took (and continue to take) vows of poverty, chastity, and obedience and follow a life of work and prayer.

Christianity for the declining fortunes of the Roman Empire. Rome in its glory days, when pagan gods and the emperors were worshipped, was militarily strong. As Christianity gained a foothold Rome found itself under the threat of extinction by invaders from the north. Some Roman citizens began to raise serious questions about the role of Christians and Christianity in the empire. Would Christians be good citizens who could be depended on to fight for Rome? Or were they so committed to Christ's kingdom that earthly kingdoms and responsibilities had no importance for them? In short, where did the Christians put their loyalty? To which kingdom did they belong—the heavenly one or the earthly one? As the debate went on Rome fell, in 410.

EARLY CHRISTIAN DIVISIONS

From its earliest days, Christianity split into various groups, each with its own beliefs and traditions. The divisions were at first about the life of Jesus, how to describe him, and how to interpret his teachings. The first major transformation was the split between the Orthodox Church in the east of the Roman Empire and the Catholic Church in the west.

Early Christianity
Christianity became the official religion of the Roman Empire in the fourth century.

Church of the East
This Church split off in 431 due to a disagreement over the title given to the Virgin Mary.

Monophysites
This group ruled that Jesus was both human and divine, two natures in one person.

The Great Schism
The Eastern and Western sections of the Roman Empire and Christianity finally split in 1054.

Orthodox
Eastern Christianity established its headquarters in Constantinople and spread east from here.

The Catholic Church
Followers of the disciple Peter established the papacy and power of the Church in Rome.

After the fall of Rome, the Catholic Church in the West could have easily fallen into a collection of small feudal churches controlled by local lords. However, the Roman papacy acted as a uniting force and prevented such a splintering. The importance of Rome had been admitted by the Eastern patriarchates, but it never grew into an acknowledgment of authority. Nor was the political ruler of the Roman Empire in Constantinople willing to admit a higher human force to which he must submit. The government of the Roman Empire was based on the idea that religious concerns were second to the interests of the empire.

GREGORY THE GREAT

Pope Gregory I, or Gregory the Great, who ruled from 590 to 604, was the first monk to become pope. The word *pope* comes from the Greek *papa* and signifies the bishop of Rome as the father figure of the whole church. The pope is the final authority within Catholicism on issues of doctrine. Popes are elected by the College of Cardinals, a group appointed by the pope and responsible for seeking the Will of the Holy Spirit through prayer and discussion as to who should be the next pope.

Gregory was not a monk totally cut off from the world. He was politically sophisticated. He had been papal representative to the imperial court at Constantinople for a number of years before his election to the papacy. His reign was outstanding. In circumstances that were very trying, he fed the poor of Rome. He managed the estates of the church in such a way that the crops were consistently abundant and the workers were treated with great humanity. He reformed church music and the celebration of worship within the church, and he preached fervently and frequently. His greatest achievement, perhaps, was his effort to bring Christianity and its message to a bigger world.

MISSIONARIES ACROSS EUROPE

In his initial effort to accomplish his mission, Gregory sent Augustine of Canterbury (d. 604) as the head of a small group of missionaries to bring Christian life and faith to England. A number of Gregory's contemporaries also carried Christianity to other parts of Europe. For example, Columban (ca. 521–97), an Irish monk, preached to the Franks. A century later Boniface (ca. 675–754) converted the Germanic peoples. In the latter part of the 10th century Christianity made rapid headway in Denmark, Sweden, and Norway. The call to baptize all nations was being accomplished.

THE FLOURISHING OF RELIGIOUS LIFE

Monastic life began to flourish, and it breathed new spiritual life into the Christianity of Rome, which then spread throughout the Western world. Benedict of Nursia (ca. 480–ca. 547) founded a number of monasteries, first at Subiaco, the mountain region east of Rome, and then in a dozen other locations. These were independent, self-supporting, and self-contained communities of monks just outside towns or in rural areas. They were dedicated to prayer, work, and study. The monastic life demands that persons withdraw from worldly affairs to devote themselves completely to religion.

DIVINE OFFICE

The houses where monks or nuns live are called abbeys, and they are ruled over by abbots (spiritual fathers) or abbesses. The life of devotion in abbeys is organized around the Divine Office. This consists of the Book of Psalms, readings from the Old and New Testaments, readings from the early church fathers, and hymns. This prayer book was structured so that all 150 psalms of the Old Testament were sung each week, with each day divided into eight parts. Every three hours a part of this Divine Office is chanted.

A SPIRIT OF PRAYER

This schedule brought to the whole day a spirit of prayer, so that even work and study were done within a prayerful atmosphere. Benedict's Rule was sturdy enough on its own, and without any common government it was able to keep order within the many independent monasteries as they multiplied. At times these monasteries became too strongly supported by the wealthy and politically powerful. Often the result was a relaxation of monastic discipline. When this happened reforms often took place, as they did at Citeaux and Cluny in France in the late 11th and early 12th centuries.

FRANCISCANS AND DOMINICANS

Other religious movements gained prominence, especially in the 12th and 13th centuries. As cities began to sprout up throughout Europe a new kind of ministry was needed besides the one carried on in the monasteries, which were usually separated from urban life. Two of the most influential movements were begun by Saint Francis of Assisi (1181–1226) and by Saint Dominic (1170–1221). They founded two religious orders, the Franciscans and the Dominicans, dedicated to poverty and preaching. The Franciscans and Dominicans also founded female communities: the Poor Claires, followers of Claire of Assisi, and the Dominican Sisters. They also established lay associates, called Third Order Franciscans or Third Order Dominicans.

THE CHRISTIAN TEACHING MISSION

In 529, the same year that Rome fell to invaders, the Benedictine monastery of Monte Cassino was founded. It was in this monastery that many of the literary and scientific works of the Roman world were copied and preserved for the future. The works of writers such as Cicero (106–43 B.C.E.), Virgil (70–19 B.C.E.), Seneca (4 B.C.E.–65 C.E.), and the many other educa-

St. Francis of Assisi is one of the most popular saints in Christian history. He is known for his life of poverty and prayer and his love of nature in which he saw the work of the Creator in all creatures. The stigmata, the marks of Christ's crucifixion on his hands and feet, were a sign of his life devoted to following the crucified Christ.

tors of Rome were copied by the monastic scribes. These works, along with the Bible, formed the building blocks of the educational reform of Charlemagne (ca. 742–814) that was headed by

THE CANTICLE OF THE CREATURES

The Canticle of the Creatures was written by Saint Francis of Assisi in praise of God and thanking him for His Creation. It reflects the personal theology of Saint Francis who often referred to animals as brothers and sisters of humanity. Most of the hymn was written in Italian in late 1224 and has since been translated into many languages.

Most high, all powerful, all good Lord! All praise is yours, all glory, all honor, and all blessing. To you, alone, Most High, do they belong. No mortal lips are worthy to pronounce your name.

Be praised, my Lord, through all your creatures, especially through my lord Brother Sun, who brings the day; and you give light through him. And he is beautiful and radiant in all his splendor! Of you, Most High, he bears the likeness.

Be praised, my Lord, through Sister Moon and the stars; in the heavens you have made them, precious and beautiful.

Be praised, my Lord, through Brothers Wind and Air, and clouds and storms, and all the weather, through which you give your creatures sustenance.

Be praised, My Lord, through Sister Water; she is very useful, and humble, and precious, and pure.

Be praised, my Lord, through Brother Fire, through whom you brighten the night. He is beautiful and cheerful, and powerful and strong.

Be praised, my Lord, through our sister Mother Earth, who feeds us and rules us, and produces various fruits with colored flowers and herbs.

Be praised, my Lord, through those who forgive for love of you; through those who endure sickness and trial. Happy those who endure in peace, for by you, Most High, they will be crowned.

Be praised, my Lord, through our Sister Bodily Death, from whose embrace no living person can escape. Woe to those who die in mortal sin! Happy those she finds doing your most holy will. The second death can do no harm to them.

Praise and bless my Lord, and give thanks, and serve him with great humility.

(Translated by Bill Barrett from the Umbrian text of the *Assisi codex*.)

the Irish monk Alcuin (735–804). Eventually schools developed that were linked to monasteries as well as to palaces and cathedrals. Monks and priests, civil clerks, and administrators were educated at these schools. Later, from some of these schools emerged the first universities located in Bologna, Paris, and Oxford.

THE MEDIEVAL PAPACY AT ITS HEIGHT

Pepin, king of the Franks from 751 to 768, helped the papacy to obtain independent territories in central Italy by fighting the Lombards, who were threatening Rome. The Franks were Germanic peoples who occupied much of France and western Germany from the sixth century onward. When Pope Leo III (795–815) conferred the imperial crown on Pepin's son, Charlemagne (800–14), thereby declaring him emperor of the Romans, he made the church independent of Constantinople and the Eastern Empire. Gregory VII (1073–85) established a system of church laws and revised papal administration so that the papacy entered upon the path of effective rulership by means of law.

The Emperor Charlemagne

Charlemagne was crowned emperor of what became known as the Holy Roman Empire by Pope Leo III on Christmas Day 800. His name means Charles the Great and he reunited much of western Europe for the first time since the fall of the Roman Empire in the fifth century.

When the first universities began as centers of Christian learning, the Franciscans and Dominicans also became strong participants in the intellectual life there. Among the most famous thinkers of the Middle Ages were Albert the Great (ca. 1200–80) and Thomas Aquinas (1224–74), both Dominicans, and Bonaventure (ca. 1217–74), Duns Scotus (1266–1308), and William of Ockham (ca. 1285–ca. 1347), who were Franciscans. These religious orders also produced well-respected preachers such as Raymond of Penafort (1185–1275), Anthony of Padua (1195–1231), Bernardine of Siena (1380–1444), and John Capistran (1385–1456).

DIVINELY INSTITUTED GOVERNMENT

The life of a Christian on earth, a life according to church law, determined life in the other world. Supporting itself by the Bible, the teachings of the church fathers, and earlier papal doctrine, the papacy established itself as the divinely instituted government of the Western Christian world. The church was the congregation of the faithful entrusted by Christ to the pope through Saint Peter and his successors. Its goal was otherworldly and none other than the holder of the keys of the kingdom of heaven knew by virtue of his office how to achieve this highest end.

REALM OF RELIGIOUS AUTHORITY

Gregory the Great had set a wonderful example for the papacy, and it was followed by many splendid instances of strong and religious popes in the 11th century: Leo IX (1048–54), Alexander II (1061–73), and Gregory VII (1073–85) are but a few. These reformers tried to keep the spiritual power of the papacy free from the control of government rulers and to separate the appointment of bishops from government powers. The 12th century also revealed many strong popes: Innocent II (1130–43), Eugene III (1145–53), Alexander II (1159–81), and Innocent III (1198–1216). They too opposed the dominance of the government rulers of their times and their invasion into the realm of religious authority. In the world of medieval papacy, a basic distinction was dominant between the office of the pope and the person of the pope. The medieval world did not consider any formula for separating the temporal from the spiritual, so both good and bad persons could hold good offices. It was the office of the pope or bishop or teacher that commanded respect even when the person holding it might detract from its dignity.

THE CRUSADES

The Crusades were a series of attempts from the 11th to the 15th centuries under the direction of the popes to free the Holy Land from the Turks. (The Holy Land covered parts of Syria, Lebanon, Jordan, and the whole of Israel and Palestine.) Initiated by Pope Urban II (1088–99) in 1095, the Crusades were portrayed as a pilgrimage and were crowned with an indulgence equal to a lifetime of penance: "If any man sets out to free the Church of God at Jerusalem out of pure devotion and not out of love for glory or gain, the journey shall be accounted a complete penance on his part." In 1099 Jerusalem was taken and the Muslim population was killed or conquered. Throughout the succeeding Crusades, however, there was dissent among the leaders and deviations from their holy purpose often led to failure. The assaults on the Muslims, and on the Greeks through whose lands they traveled during these attempts to rescue the Holy Land, have left deep-rooted hatreds even to the present.

THE MEDIEVAL INQUISITION

Inquisitions were instituted by the popes. Pope Gregory IX (1227–41) established the Medieval Inquisition in 1229 to try

A portion of a painting of the siege and capture of Antioch by the Crusaders from the Muslim Seljuks who had been in control of the city for two years. The Siege of Antioch took place during the First Crusade with the capture of the city by the Crusaders after a campaign that lasted from October 21, 1097 until June 2, 1098. A second siege then followed that same June as the Crusaders defended Antioch.

to destroy those people they believed to be heretics. One such group, the Albigensians, admitted two principles as the source of the universe: a good principle that created spiritual reality and a bad principle that created material things. Their way of life and dress was simple, and they attacked the worldliness of the clergy. They also rejected the Old Testament and opposed infant baptism, since it lacked a personal commitment to Christ. Condemned at the Council of Albi in 1176, they continued to survive. Pope Gregory created a powerful body that had almost unlimited powers to persecute those it considered to be heretics. The brutal use of the Inquisition, combined with a war against the Albigensians, led to the mass murder of thousands in the south of France. The Inquisition was also used in the early 14th century to destroy the Knights Templar, who were accused of heresy, and was used against the Waldensians—an early Protestant group who rejected the power of the clergy and who created new communities in the mountains of northern Italy from the 13th century onward.

THE SPANISH INQUISITION

More than 200 years later, in 1478, a different form of inquisition was founded by Ferdinand (1452–1516) and Isabella (1451–1504) in Spain. The Spanish Inquisition was a more pronouncedly civil instrument. It was used to persecute those Jews and Muslims who had been forcibly converted to Christianity at the end of the 15th century but whom the church never trusted. It was essentially an arm of the Spanish state, designed to destroy all who might think or act differently. The English were horrified by the Inquisition, and so they were particularly joyful when they defeated the Spanish Armada in 1588, which Catholic king of Spain, Philip, had sent to England.

DIVISIONS AMONG THE CHRISTIAN CHURCHES OF THE WEST

Splits from the Catholic Church continued in the West. Differing opinions and views once again caused problems among Christians. Does God save us without our efforts? Or do we merit heaven by our own good works? Is the Bible alone a sufficient guide for a Christian, or is the Catholic Church the divinely appointed authority for interpreting its message?

The Christian world of the Catholic Church was also confronted with new ideas and possibilities through the discovery of the New World of America. This brought many issues to the fore, such as what was the spiritual nature of people like the Native Americans, and how should the church treat them? The Renaissance—the eruption of ancient learning into the late medieval world that challenged many long-cherished beliefs about the world, also confronted the church with worldviews that did not fit the classical medieval Christian views.

MARTIN LUTHER

Martin Luther (1483–1546), an Augustinian monk, raised such issues. On October 31, 1517, he nailed the 95 theses to the door of Wittenberg Cathedral in Germany. In the document, he accused the Roman Catholic Church of being too involved with political and material ambition. In his pamphlet "On Christian Liberty" he established the division between the political and spiritual, the natural and the supernatural, the human and the divine. According to Luther the Roman Church had compromised too much with this world. It had blurred the distinction between political and religious power with its theory of merit by human efforts and by its doctrine on indulgences, which allowed people to use money to obtain forgiveness and heavenly rewards.

REFORM MOVEMENTS

The religious world, according to Luther, should be more spiritual and less worldly. Luther's basic premise was that religion should always be criticizing those who are attached to worldly things and earthly power. Many other efforts at reform, frequently with separating tendencies, followed Luther's lead. Ulrich Zwingli (1484–1531), Guillaume Farel (1489–1565), Martin Bucer (1491–1551), and John Calvin (1509–64) all preached reform and eventually separated from the Roman Church. Even Roman Catholicism itself began to seek reform from within.

CATHOLIC REFORMATION

The Catholic Church throughout its history often sought reform for its infidelities to the Gospel teachings. This is evident from the reforms of Benedictine life in the 11th and 12th centuries at Citeau and Cluny in France. Bernard of Clairvaux (1090–1153), less than 20 years after the founding of the Cistercian Order at Citeau in 1098, was pushing for even further reforms of Citeau. For Bernard the monks had too many associations with rich supporters. He attacked the ornateness of their cloisters: "If the monks are engrossed in their reading [of the Scriptures], what is the purpose of these ludicrous monstrosities, this incredibly distorted beauty and perfection of ugliness?" He felt that monasteries need not mimic castles.

CHURCH LAWS IN THE MIDDLE AGES

The need for church reform on a broader level was also clear from the church laws that were developed throughout the Middle Ages to guide and direct the life and activities of the church. In Italy during the 14th century Girolamo Savonarola (1452–98) preached against church abuses, as did Francisco Ximenes (1436–1517) in Spain. Pope Adrian VI (1522–23) admitted that corruption had touched even the highest levels of the prelates and clergy. In 1542 Pope Paul III (1534–49) called for a General Council of the Church at Trent to express more clearly the teachings of the church and to institute reform in the religious life of its members. This council attempted to state the differences between Catholic and Protestant teachings. It also established seminaries or schools for the training of priests in correct Catholic teaching and

ECUMENICAL COUNCILS OF THE CHURCH

The first seven councils are recognized as such by the Orthodox and Catholic churches. The remaining councils are recognized only by the Catholic Church:

Nicaea I	325
Constantinople I	381
Ephesus	432
Chalcedon	451
Constantinople II	553
Constantinople III	680–81
Nicaea II	787
Constantinople IV	869–70
Lateran I (Rome)	1123
Lateran II	1139
Lateran III	1179
Lateran IV	1215
Lyons I	1245
Lyons II	1274
Vienne (France)	1311–12
Constance	1414–18
Basle-Ferrara-Florence	1431–45
Lateran V	1512–17
Trent	1545–63
Vatican I	1869–70
Vatican II	1962–65

exemplary living. During his pontificate Paul III also gave formal approval to the Society of Jesus, the Jesuit order founded by Ignatius of Loyola (1491–1556) in 1534. The Jesuits played a leading role in the church's program of spiritual renewal.

CHALLENGES TO CATHOLICISM FROM THE SEVENTEENTH TO THE NINETEENTH CENTURIES

Despite the strong and successful efforts of the church to renew Christian life among its members new challenges to the church kept arising. The conflicts between Catholic and Protestant citizens in European countries discredited the church, and now all Christian traditions began to be questioned.

"ON TOLERATION"

Toleration of religious differences was appealed to by the philosopher John Locke (1632–1704) in his essay "On Toleration," written during his exile from England in the 1680s. The basic assumptions of Locke's work are that the teachings of any church are opinions that people hold, and every reasonable opinion should be respected. He argued that people simply choose to join a religion the way they choose to belong to any organization. Religious gatherings and celebrations are permitted on the same terms as a dinner meeting of an extended family or a club. In short, religious rituals are treated in the same way as a secular event: A Eucharistic liturgy in Locke's view is simply an act of eating bread and wine. Catholics claim that during the Mass the bread and wine become the body and blood of Christ (a process called transfiguration). Locke would later claim that Catholics have a right to believe such a thing as long as it does not harm anyone.

Galileo

The rise of science and of philosophical inquiry, rooted in the Renaissance and flourishing in the new intellectual world of the 16th to 19th centuries, threatened the Catholic worldview. Galileo, who in the 1630s published the first full explanation that the sun was at the center of the solar system (countering the belief of the church that the earth was at the center) was persecuted by the Inquisition and forced to take back his statement. It was only at the end of the 20th century that the pope apologized for this action.

THE AGE OF REASON

Other writers, such as Swiss-born Jean-Jacques Rousseau (1712–78) in *The Social Contract* of 1762, likewise promoted the religion during a time in Europe that came to be called the Age of Reason. Rousseau argued for a secular religion that would alone be beneficial to society and would avoid the conflicts often engendered by Catholic or Protestant faiths. His religion would have just a few tenets that all people of goodwill would surely accept: There is a God who exists, and he is all-knowing. We have souls that survive death. God rewards the good and punishes the wicked, including those who do not live up to the obligations of their contracts.

APPOINTMENT BY KINGS

The desire on the part of kings, especially in France, to control the appointment of bishops, brought great tensions between popes and kings. Kings started to appoint the bishops in the territories they controlled, which undermined papal influence. Under such conditions the church in these countries became a puppet of the king. As democracy and revolution attacked the king they also began to attack the church, whose hierarchy had been appointed by the king.

THE CATHOLIC RESPONSE

The leadership of the church was strengthened under two long-reigning popes in the second half of the 19th century. Pope Pius IX (1846–78), who convened the First Vatican Council (1869–70), reestablished respect for the papacy. The council managed to restore the teaching authority of the papacy by declaring the pope to be infallible regarding matters of the church. This meant he would be the ultimate authority on religious questions and debates. This helped ensure the independence of the church in the spiritual realm from the control of secular rulers. However, this reactionary stance of the papacy was not welcomed by all Catholics and created divisions between traditionalists and modernists that continue to this day.

ADDRESSING THE MODERN WORLD

Pius's successor, Leo XIII (1878–1903), made strong efforts to convince liberal secular leaders that they and the church could live in harmony. He tried to deal with the modern world on many levels. In education he proclaimed Thomas Aquinas as a solid example of Catholic thinking that could deal well with the challenges presented by modern philosophers like Locke and Rousseau. On another level Leo XIII kept close contact with everyday problems of ordinary Catholics and addressed them through letters. These encyclical letters, or letters addressed to the universal church, often dealt with social issues that touched the daily lives of Catholic working people. Through his stimulation Roman Catholicism became even more socially active.

THE MODERN CATHOLIC RESPONSE TO SOCIAL ISSUES

At the end of the 19th and the beginning of the 20th centuries, the church responded to the needs of the large number of poor immigrants who needed assistance in getting food, housing, and work in their new homeland of the United States. As a result, the church that seemed to be losing influence in a number of secular societies in Europe began gaining in numbers and dedication in lands outside of Europe. With the wave of immigrants from Ireland, Italy, southern Germany, Poland, Portugal, and Spain, for example, Roman Catholicism began to have strong influence once again, this time in North America.

The bread and wine consecrated by the priest during a Catholic Eucharist are believed to become the body and blood of Christ.

SECOND VATICAN COUNCIL

The Catholic Church took its most dramatic step in its effort to relate to modern secular culture and other religions at the Second Vatican Council. This council, which lasted from 1962 to 1965, was initiated by Pope John XXIII (1958–63) and was completed by Pope Paul VI (1963–78). Its important document, the *Constitution on the Church,* gave ordinary people a greater active role in church life and granted bishops a greater share in the authority of the church. Pope John Paul II (1978–2005), who grew up under Communist rule in Poland, continued to promote a more active involvement of the Catholic Church in society. He made frequent visits to his flocks throughout the world, particularly addressing young Catholics, whom he viewed as the flourishing future of the church.

THE HISTORY OF THE EASTERN CHURCHES

Tensions between the Eastern churches and Rome arose shortly after the Roman Empire was separated into eastern and western halves at the end of the third century. Each part of the empire eventually had its own emperor and language. The East spoke Greek and the West spoke Latin. These political and linguistic differences have made attempts at union difficult throughout history, and the split still remains.

SEPARATION OF CATHOLIC AND ORTHODOX CHURCHES

The first real, although still partial, split came with the Nestorian and Monophysite heresies condemned at the Councils of Ephesus (431) and Chalcedon (451). A much more serious separation occurred in 1054, when the Eastern churches and Rome mutually excommunicated each other—ending recognition of the validity of the other as a proper church. The two main issues involved in this separation were the primacy of the pope and the manner of explaining the doctrine of the Trinity. The Orthodox accepted the pope as the most honored bishop of the Christian world, but he was still one bishop among many. They thus did not believe that the pope should have direct authority over all Christians.

QUESTIONS AND DISAGREEMENTS

The Orthodox Church also refused to accept the Catholic change made to the Nicene/Constantinople Creed concerning the relationship of the Holy Spirit to the Father and the Son. For the Eastern churches the Holy Spirit proceeds from the Father alone. The Catholic Church declares that the Holy Spirit proceeds from the Father and the Son, Jesus. The disagreements became so intense that they led to the mutual excommunication of the patriarch of Constantinople, the head of the Orthodox Church, and the papal legate representing the power and authority of the pope as head of the Western Church. The lengthy process of estrangement continued until it culminated in a complete split upon the sack of Orthodox Constantinople by the Catholic Crusaders in 1204.

"APOSTLES OF THE SLAVS"

The center of Eastern Christianity increasingly shifted northward to the Slavic countries. The conversion of the Slavs to Eastern Christianity began in the ninth century through the missionary work of two Greek brothers, Cyril (ca. 827–69) and Methodius (ca. 825–85). As a result of their efforts Eastern Christianity

An iconostasis decorated with figures of Christ, the mother of God, and saints in the Russian Orthodox monastery of Valaam in Karelia, northern Russia. In an Orthodox church the iconostasis is the screen separating the nave from the altar.

spread to Bulgaria, Serbia, and Russia. Cyril and Methodius are thus recognized in the Eastern tradition as "apostles of the Slavs." Eastern Christianity became the official state religion of Russia in 988 with the conversion of Prince Vladimir of Kiev (956–1015). Vladimir was a devoted Christian who tried to rule his country in a Christian manner, initiating the ideal of a "holy Russia." Monasteries and Christian culture thrived under his rule. The tradition of icon painting flourished during that time. One of the most famous religious images of Christendom is the icon of the Holy Trinity by Saint Andrei Rublev (ca. 1360–1430).

The domes of Troitse Sergieva (Holy Trinity monastery), which lies northeast of Moscow, was founded by Saint Sergius in 1345. This monastery has been the center of Russian Orthodoxy for hundreds of years and is an important center of theological study and religious education. After the Russian Revolution of 1917 the monastery was closed down; it was returned to the Russian Orthodox Church in 1945.

ORTHODOX CHRISTIANITY IN THE MIDDLE AGES

Orthodox Christianity maintained and developed its own distinctive approach to Christian life. An important development of Orthodox Christianity in the Middle Ages was the movement of "quietness." This practice began with Orthodox monks who engaged in continual efforts at placing themselves in the presence of Jesus. Often they would do this by praying the "Jesus prayer": "Lord Jesus Christ, Son of the living God, have mercy on me, a sinner." Many of these monks claimed that they had attained a certain union with God through these exercises, purging themselves of other concerns. Others criticized them, insisting that God could not be directly experienced.

One of the great figures of the Orthodox Christian tradition, Saint Gregory Palamas (1296–1359), resolved the issue by explaining that although we cannot participate in God's being, people can experience God's energies, or grace, operating in them. Orthodox Christians to this day place a great value on meditating on the Jesus prayer. They often use a prayer rope, which looks much like a rosary, to assist them in this practice.

From the early centuries of Christianity to the 15th century the center of Orthodox Christianity was Constantinople. However, in 1453 Constantinople was captured by the Muslim Turks. The Greek Constantinople became the Turkish Istanbul. Orthodox Christians continued to live and practice their faith under the Turkish rule of the Ottoman Empire but they were made to pay special taxes, and the spread of their faith was curtailed since any form of missionary activity was forbidden.

MAJOR EASTERN CATHOLIC CHURCHES

The following is a list of some major Eastern Catholic churches and the dates of their reunion with the Church of Rome:

Ukrainian Catholic Church: 1595
Ruthenian Catholic Church: 1646
Syrian Catholic Church: 1656
Melkite Catholic Church: 1724
Armenian Catholic Church: 1742
Chaldean Catholic Church (present-day Iraq): 1834
Coptic (Egyptian) Catholic Church: 1899

All of the above Catholic churches have Orthodox counterparts. Among the other Eastern Catholic churches are the Syro-Malankara Catholic Church and the Syro-Malabar Catholic Church, both in India; the Romanian Catholic Church; the Bulgarian Catholic Church; the Slovak Catholic Church; and the Hungarian Catholic Church.

THE EASTERN CATHOLIC CHURCHES

Eastern Catholic churches came into existence when groups of Orthodox Christians sought reunion with the Church of Rome after the division between East and West in 1054. Eastern Catholics have the same religious practices as the Orthodox, and they share the same history as their counterparts in the Orthodox churches up to the point when they established their reunion with Rome. Eastern Catholics recognize the pope as the ultimate spiritual authority. Some Eastern Catholic churches do not have an Orthodox counterpart and have always maintained communion with Rome. Such is the case with the Maronite Catholic Church, which is the major Christian church of Lebanon.

At the Second Vatican Council, a general council of the Catholic Church held at Vatican City from 1962 to 1965, in the Decree on Eastern Catholic Churches and the Decree on the Ministry and Life of Priests, the council reasserted the equality of Eastern Catholic churches with the Latin Rite. While stressing that an unmarried way of life was a necessary requirement for Latin Rite priests, it did not change the discipline that allowed married priests in the Eastern Rite Catholic churches.

MODERN CHALLENGES TO THE ORTHODOX CHURCHES

Different challenges have been presented to the various Orthodox churches in the 20th century. The Russian Revolution of 1917 and the rise of the Communist Party caused great suffering and confusion in Russia. It also caused a split among Russian Orthodox Christians. In 1920 some Orthodox Russians who were in exile from their homeland instituted an independent church that came to be known as the Russian Orthodox Church Outside Russia. They elected their own bishop in defiance of the Soviet appointees. In 2007 the Russian Orthodox Church and the Russian Orthodox Church Outside Russia reunited, to great joy from all sides. Other Orthodox churches have suffered similar divisions based on different views. For example questions have arisen, such as whether the Orthodox churches should engage in

A detail from a mosaic depicting Mary, the mother of God,
and Christ, the son of God. This is one of the remaining
mosaics in Hagia Sophia, the great church built by Emperor
Justinian I in 537 in Constantinople (present-day Istanbul).

The ecumenical patriarch of Constantinople, Bartholomew, ceremonially plants a tree as part of an Orthodox gathering to highlight and celebrate Orthodox involvement in environmental issues. The ecumenical patriarch is the leading figure of the Orthodox Church. Although there are other Orthodox patriarchs, he is recognized as the first among equals.

dialogue with other Christian churches (ecumenism), or whether they should base their liturgical year on the old Julian calendar, named after Julius Caesar (100–44 B.C.E.) and authoritative for Eastern countries, or on the new "Gregorian" calendar, named after Pope Gregory XIII (1572–85) that has been adopted over the years by most modern civil governments.

ORTHODOXY OUTSIDE RUSSIA

Outside of Russia all the main Orthodox churches have suffered persecution in the 20th century, whether from nationalism that took away their lands or from Communist rule. The destruction of religious life and its associated customs and traditions, and of people, buildings, and artifacts across the Orthodox world is greater than at any other time in their history. However, once Communism fell in the 1980s the church was able to rebuild itself swiftly and efficiently, and has emerged in many of the Orthodox countries—for example Russia, Georgia, Serbia, and Romania—as a major social force.

ORTHODOXY IN THE UNITED STATES

In the United States political and cultural disagreements between home countries gradually seemed artificial to church members. Movements were formed to rise above ethnic differences. New churches were formed that attempted to make their communities more American or more ecumenical. Such an attempt is the Orthodox Church of America, whose membership has now reached over a million.

In the United States many Orthodox Christians are now engaged in an effort to unite all American Orthodox Christians into one church that transcends ethnic boundaries and seeks to communicate the rich traditions of Orthodoxy in the common language of American culture. Still, particular Orthodox churches in America continue to flourish. A good example is the Greek Orthodox Church. It has founded its own college, Hellenic College, in Boston, and despite strong competition from non-Greek schools, it has continued to draw a consistent student body. Its seminary has a respected faculty that is part of the theological cooperative called the Boston Theological Consortium.

CATHOLIC AND ORTHODOX ATTEMPTS AT UNITY

In recent decades many efforts have been made to foster dialogue and unity between Catholic and Orthodox Christians. Popes and patriarchs have started to visit each other and to send fraternal greetings at special festival times in each other's calendars. For example Pope Paul VI, following up on his previous attempts to reach out to Orthodox Christians, invited the Coptic, or Egyptian, Orthodox leader Shenouda III to visit the Vatican in 1973. He was the first Coptic leader in over 1,500 years to visit Rome. Pope John Paul II also made frequent attempts to establish contact with various leaders of the Orthodox churches.

RESTORING CHRISTIAN UNITY

At the invitation of the Romanian Orthodox patriarch Teocist, who had visited Rome 10 years earlier, the pope came to Romania in May 1999. After meeting with the Catholic bishops there, he also met with the 36 Orthodox bishops of that country. These attempts at reconciliation with the Eastern Christian world were undertaken with hope, and also with a realistic sense of the historical events that have kept these churches separated for nearly a thousand years. The sense of hope was well expressed in the welcoming remarks of Patriarch Teocist: "The second millennium of Christian history began with a painful wounding of the unity of the church; the end of this millennium has seen a real commitment to restoring Christian unity."

CHALLENGES TO UNITY

The task of restoring that unity, however, poses many real challenges. The visit of Pope John Paul II in 1999 raised fears in Romania, and also in Russia, that the pope was meddling in internal Orthodox affairs, supporting an independent Romanian Orthodox Church that wanted to separate from the influence of the Moscow patriarchate. Others interpreted the pope's visit as part of a push by Rome to get back property that belonged to the Romanian Catholic Church. The property had been confiscated by the Russians under the reign of Joseph Stalin and given to the Romanian Orthodox Church that was united with the Moscow patriarchate. Many others saw it as an honest gesture on the part of the pope to promote the unity of the churches.

Pope Benedict XVI continued the ecumenical efforts of his predecessors. In November 2005 he accepted an invitation from

Pope Benedict XVI on a pastoral visit to Bavaria, Germany, shortly after his election to the papacy in April 2005. Pope Benedict XVI was born in 1927 in the diocese of Passau in Germany. The pope is continuing ecumenical dialogue and moves toward unity with the Orthodox Church.

the Orthodox metropolitans who attended his inauguration as pope to visit the Phanar district of Istanbul, the seat of the patriarchate of the Orthodox Church in Turkey. He thus follows in the footsteps of Pope Paul VI, who visited Phanar in July 1967, and Pope John Paul II, who visited in 1979, the year after he became pope. In December 2006, Archbishop Christodoulos, archbishop of Athens, visited the pope. It was the first official visit to the Vatican by a leader of the Greek Orthodox Church. These repeated pushes for dialogue and unity inflame the hopes of many Catholic and Orthodox believers. Still, a knowledge of the history of the relations between the Eastern and Western Churches and a knowledge of the structures and traditions helps put into perspective the challenging complexities that any such attempts at unity must face.

Pope Benedict XVI Visits the United States

In 2008, Pope Benedict visited the United States, where his visit was expected to be controversial. This was because of the sexual scandals that caused great distress to Catholics in the United States and because of the opposition of the pope to the United States-led invasion of Iraq. In the end, as with his later visit in August to the World Youth Congress in Australia, Pope Benedict managed to develop strong relationships without compromising his position. He condemned outright the sexual abuse of children that was the cause of the scandals, and stood firm on his opposition to the war in Iraq.

CHAPTER 4

CATHOLICISM AND ORTHODOX CHRISTIANITY: BASIC BELIEFS AND PRACTICES

Both the Catholic and Orthodox churches greatly value doctrine, which is a set of beliefs that describes the community's experience of God's revelation and salvation. They hold that these beliefs are ultimately derived from the Bible as it has been interpreted through church councils, the teachings of the ancient fathers of the church, and short statements of belief called creeds (such as the Apostle's Creed and the Nicene Creed). For Catholics and Orthodox Christians tradition provides the authoritative interpretation of scripture. The two central doctrines, or beliefs, of Christianity are the following truths, which are affirmed in all the creeds accepted by the Catholic and Orthodox churches:

- the belief that although there is only one God, there are three persons (Father, Son, and Holy Spirit) in God;

Christian pilgrims of various denominations gathered close to the Holy Sepulchre in Jerusalem on Good Friday. They are taking part in the Stations of the Cross, recalling Christ's final journey through Jerusalem on the day of his crucifixion.

• the belief that the Son of God became human.

God thus was incarnated, meaning that he took on human flesh or became human in the person of Jesus Christ. The first belief—the belief in the Holy Trinity—was revealed by Christ, who spoke of his father and promised the apostles that he would send the Holy Spirit. In his life and teachings, in the miracles that he worked, and in his resurrection from the dead, Jesus Christ was revealed to his disciples as divine. Jesus thus taught his disciples to experience God as threefold, as Father, Son, and Holy Spirit. The disciples prayed to each as God, because they recognized that the three are united in being and are one God.

THE DOCTRINE OF THE TRINITY

Both Catholics and Orthodox Christians adhere to this doctrine of God. The Eastern liturgy suggests how God as three persons can be experienced to some small degree by thinking about love: "Let us love one another in order that we may confess the Father, the Son, and the Holy Spirit, Trinity, one in being, and undivided." If we love someone we are united with them in a special way. Since God is perfect, then his love will also be perfect. The union among the persons in God will thus be so perfect that they will be united as one.

THE DOCTRINE OF SIN

For Catholics and Orthodox Christians humanity was created for the purpose of sharing in God's own life. They believe that God ordained this purpose for humanity when he created people according to his own image and likeness, as is told in Genesis, the first book of the Bible. However, for Catholics and Orthodox Christians the sin of disobedience to God's command by the first man, Adam, interfered with God's plan. By disobeying God, human beings lost their way and became inclined to further disobedience and sin. Catholics speak of this condition as "original sin," which means that everyone is born into the world with some inclination toward sin.

A MERCIFUL RESPONSE

While the Christian Bible recounts the story of human sinfulness throughout history, it depicts God's primary response to human sinfulness as one of mercy. Catholics and Orthodox Christians believe that the greatest act of God's mercy occurred when God sent his own son into our human condition. They believe that God the Son became human, not by losing his divinity, but by combining his divinity with our humanity. Jesus Christ is one person who contains both divine and human natures. This combination healed humanity and transformed it into a humanity that is empowered by divine life.

A NEW LIFE IN BELIEF

By dying on the cross Christ killed the power of death and destroyed the root of evil. By his resurrection, he showed the victory of God over death and evil and the new life that is now open to all those who believe in him. Catholics and Orthodox Christians believe that this new life can be shared by all his followers through faith and through participation in the sacraments of the church. This is a process that begins on earth. It is only completed after death. Thus they say in their creed (statement of beliefs): "We believe in the Resurrection of the dead and the life of the world to come."

THE IMPORTANCE OF SAINTS

Roman Catholics and Orthodox Christians place great importance and value on honoring saints. To Catholics saints are persons who have led exceptionally holy lives and who have been formally recognized by the church as having achieved an honored position in heaven. This entitles them to respect and devotion on earth. For Orthodox churches saints are likewise holy people recognized as such by their community. Orthodoxy does not have the saint-making structures and requirements

The Hail Mary (Ave Maria)

Hail Mary, full of grace, The Lord is with thee. Blessed art thou amongst women, and blessed is the fruit of thy womb, Jesus. Holy Mary, Mother of God, pray for us sinners now and at the hour of our death. Amen.

Paintings of saints on the walls of an 11th-century Christian church in Cappadocia, Turkey. For many Catholics and Orthodox Christians the saints are examples to imitate and from whom to draw inspiration. Statues of the saints are often prominently displayed in Catholic churches, as are icons (religious images) of saints in Orthodox and Eastern Catholic churches.

of the Catholic Church, trusting its local congregations to be wise in their evaluation of saints.

In the Catholic and Orthodox traditions the greatest of the saints is considered to be Mary, the mother of Jesus. Because they believe that Jesus Christ is God, Mary is referred to as the "Mother of God." Since Christ did not have a human father but "by the power of the Holy Spirit was born of Mary," Mary is also referred to as the Blessed Virgin. The special nature of her motherhood is told in the Gospel of Luke (1:26–38), where the angel Gabriel tells Mary that she will conceive the son of God by the power of the Holy Spirit. The faith of the Catholic and Orthodox Churches finds great significance in Mary's role as the mother of Jesus. According to this teaching, when Mary became the moth-

er of Jesus, she also became the mother of the church itself that descended from him.

In the Gospel of John Jesus tells his beloved disciple John that he is now to consider Mary his own mother: "When Jesus saw his mother and the disciple whom he loved standing beside her, he said to his mother, 'Woman, here is your son.' Then he said to the disciple, 'Here is your mother.' And from that hour the disciple took her into his own home." (John 19:26–27)

WORSHIP AND LITURGY

The public acts of worship that Catholics and Orthodox Christians perform together are called the liturgy. For Catholics and Orthodox the central act of the liturgy is the Eucharist, generally referred to as "Mass" in the Roman Catholic tradition and "Divine Liturgy" in the Orthodox tradition. The liturgy of most of the Eastern Catholic churches is also referred to as the "Byzantine Liturgy," because it originated in the Eastern part of the Roman Empire, called Byzantium. It is also known as the Liturgy of Saint John Chrysostom, who was a saint and bishop of the early church and is thought to have composed many of the prayers of this liturgy.

Weekly attendance at Sunday liturgy and attendance on special feast days such as Christmas is required of all church members. These are called holy days of obligation in the Catholic Church. In addition Catholics carry out acts of devotion to Mary and the saints, such as novenas—devotions consisting of prayers or services held on nine consecutive days or weeks. Orthodox Christians also have special services honoring Mary and her role in Christ's work of salvation. These are called Akathist, which is a Greek word meaning "standing," referring to the fact

A Special Relationship to Christ

For Catholics and Orthodox Christians devotion to Mary is always in the context of her special relationship to Christ. The following prayer expresses the joyous affirmation of this special relationship:

In you, Virgin, full of grace,
all creation does rejoice,
all the orders of angels and
all of the human race.
God who lives eternally
took his human flesh from thee.
And he made your womb a throne
wider than the heavenly places . . .

ICONS IN ORTHODOX CHURCHES

In the Orthodox tradition great value is placed on the role of icons, representations in paint or enamel of sacred personages such as Christ or the saints. The icons themselves are venerated and considered sacred. The Orthodox Christian doctrine of icons grows out of the belief that the incarnation of God in Jesus Christ has made it possible for all material reality to be an instrument for the revelation of God's glory. Icons are not considered to be just paintings but are viewed as communicating the presence of the person or persons whom they represent. A great Orthodox theologian, Saint John of Damascus, put it this way: "I shall not cease reverencing matter, by means of which my salvation has been achieved."

that the congregation traditionally stands while chanting the praises of Mary.

In the Orthodox Church there is a tradition of sacred icons, which are painted or enamelled representations of holy figures such as Christ, Mary and the saints. The icons are considered sacred because they are a means by which the worshipper can communicate in prayer and spirit with the religious figures represented in the icon.

THE CHURCH CALENDAR

In both the Orthodox and Catholic traditions liturgical prayer and piety are organized with a view to the seasons of the liturgical year. Throughout history Christianity saw a progression in the development of liturgical observances. In the early years of Christianity many Chris-

A portable home icon showing Mary the Mother of God, God the Father, and Jesus the Son of God. The icons are in a small case that can be easily carried and opened for prayer.

tians assumed that the Second Coming of Christ was near and that the world would soon come to an end. The Second Coming is the belief that Jesus will return at the end of the world to create a new heaven and a new earth. Until the fourth century the church formally celebrated only Sundays, Easter, and Pentecost; holy days related to the redemption of humanity. As Christians began to accept that the world had not come to an end and was unlikely to come to an end any time soon, they also accepted as a reminder of ideal Christian life on earth a calendar of feast days that had been developed informally. By the Middle Ages each day of the year honored a saint, an event, or a religious reality such as the Trinity.

Christian holy days often transformed traditional pagan, or pre-Christian, festivals. For example, ceremonies and symbols associated with the vernal equinox—the beginning of spring— took on new depth and meaning and came to represent Christ's resurrection. December 25th was celebrated in ancient Rome as the feast of Sol Invictus, the unconquered sun. Kindling the Yule log, decorating houses with holly and evergreens, and adorning an evergreen tree were magical pagan acts to encourage the sun's return. For Christians Christ is the light of the world, the spiritual sun. Christians gave the ancient pagan feast a new meaning, and many pagan symbols were converted to express different facets of the new Christian meaning.

SPECIAL FEASTS AND FESTIVALS

At present both the Catholic and Orthodox churches have liturgical calendars marked by the observance of many feasts and festivals. Nevertheless the most important of these are still the ones that commemorate the major events in the life of Jesus Christ. In the Catholic tradition the liturgical year begins in Advent, the time of preparation for the celebration of Christmas.

LENT AND EASTER

Not long after the celebration of Christmas the time of Lent begins, a time of preparation for the celebration of the death and resurrection of Christ during Holy Week. Lent, beginning with Ash Wednesday and extending for a period of 40 days, is considered to be a time of purification and sacrifice. Ash Wednesday is given this name because believers mark their faces with ash to show their sorrow for their sins at the start of this period of reflection and repentance.

During Lent, it is customary to give up something one enjoys, such as sweets or television, as a sign of repentance and single-minded dedication to God. Additionally, it is expected that Catholics abstain from meat on Fridays. After Easter comes the celebration of Pentecost, the descent of the Holy Spirit upon the apostles. As well as the Advent, Christmas, Lent, and Easter

seasons, the Catholic liturgical calendar also contains a period called ordinary time. This time is often interpreted as the season for focusing on how the life of Christ can be applied to one's own life in the world today.

MAJOR ORTHODOX FEASTS

The same major feasts as the Catholic tradition are celebrated in the Orthodox tradition, where the liturgical year begins on September 1. The Orthodox tradition places much emphasis on preparation for the major feasts of Christmas and especially Easter. Some form of fasting is prescribed for the period preceding both feasts. The traditional Lenten fast includes abstaining from

A community procession in Warsaw, Poland, celebrating the feast day of Corpus Christi (the body of Christ). In the Catholic calendar this holy day commemorates the Eucharist as the body of Christ and is celebrated on the Thursday following the first Sunday after Pentecost.

FEASTS OF THE CATHOLIC AND ORTHODOX CHURCHES

Among the most important universal church observances shared by both the Catholic and Orthodox Churches are:

Lent (period beginning 40 weekdays before Easter): an annual season of fasting and penitence in preparation for Easter.

Palm Sunday (Sunday before Easter): commemorates Christ's triumphal entry into Jerusalem.

Holy Thursday (Thursday before Easter): celebrates Jesus's gift of his body and blood in the Eucharist; the anniversary of the Last Supper.

Good Friday (Friday before Easter): the commemoration of the crucifixion of Christ.

Easter Sunday (Sunday after Good Friday): celebrates Jesus Christ's resurrection from the dead.

Ascension Day (40th day after Easter): celebrates the ascension, or rising of Christ to heaven.

Pentecost (seventh Sunday after Easter): commemorates the descent of the Holy Spirit on the disciples.

Assumption of Mary (known as "Dormition of Mary" in the Eastern churches; August 15th): celebrates the day on which God assumed the body of Mary into heaven.

Immaculate Conception (December 8th): celebrates the sinlessness of Mary, the mother of Christ. (Eastern Christians also recognize the sinlessness of Mary, but do not speak of it in these terms. The birth of Mary is celebrated on this day in the Eastern Churches as the Conception of Saint Anne, the day on which Mary was conceived by Anne, her mother.)

Christmas (December 25th): celebrates the birth of Christ.

all meat and dairy products, as well as intensified prayer and almsgiving. The highlight of the Orthodox liturgical year is Easter, the Feast of the Resurrection of Christ, in which the faithful sing repeatedly:

Christ is risen from the dead
trampling down death by death
and upon those in the tomb
bestowing life.

DIVINE LITURGY AND MASS

The festive character of any holy day, as well as that of regular Sundays, is centered on the celebration of the Eucharist. In both the Catholic and Orthodox traditions this celebration has two main parts, the Liturgy of the Word and the Eucharistic Liturgy.

LITURGY OF THE WORD

In both traditions the liturgy of the word consists of a petition for forgiveness of sins, hymns, prayers, biblical readings, a homily or sermon concerning the biblical readings, and a declaration of faith through the recitation of the creed. The biblical readings generally follow a pattern of presenting three related texts. One text is from the Old Testament, another from the Letters of the New Testament, and the last from one of the four Gospels. The readings also follow a cycle, so that a broad collection of scriptural readings is heard over a number of years. Listeners thus encounter the fullness of divine revelation. The homily is not intended to be a sermon covering any subject the priest might choose, but is meant to be an exposition of the contents of the three texts.

"What shall we offer thee?"

Beautiful prayers are a feature of the Orthodox tradition, such as this one for Christmas Day, which celebrates how all of creation contributed something to the Incarnation:

What shall we offer Thee, O Christ, who for our sake was seen on earth as man? For everything created by Thee offers Thee thanks. The angels offer Thee their hymn; the heavens, the star; the Magi, their gifts; the shepherds, their wonder; the earth, the cave; the wilderness, the manger; while we offer Thee a Virgin Mother, O pre-eternal God, have mercy upon us . . ."

—Hymn for vespers, Christmas Day

THE EUCHARISTIC LITURGY

The Eucharistic Liturgy is a celebration of the Lord's Supper, also known as the Last Supper—the meal Jesus shared with his disciples the evening before his crucifixion. In many ways the structure of the Mass follows the Passover meal or seder that Christ shared with his disciples. Gifts of bread and wine are offered to God. The priest, acting in Jesus's name and invoking the power of the Holy Spirit, changes these gifts into Christ's body and blood. The congregation then receives, under the appearance of bread and wine, the body and blood of Christ. The Catholic and Orthodox churches teach firmly that the Eucharist involves an actual change. Its members believe in faith that the sacrament is not just a symbol of Christ's body and blood; it is the body and blood of Christ. For Catholics and Orthodox Christians the Eucharist or Divine Liturgy is a participation in the life of Christ. They believe that the church participates in the heavenly Kingdom of God through the Divine Liturgy.

THE SEVEN SACRAMENTS

The seven sacraments are present in both Catholic and Orthodox churches. They are ceremonial signs of God's action in people's lives.

THE SACRAMENTS

Important liturgical acts of Catholic and Orthodox Christians include the sacraments. The word *sacrament* means "seal." The sacraments seal the relationship between God and the Christian community. The seven sacraments, which are all present in both Catholic and Orthodox churches, are ceremonial signs of God's action in people's lives. Catholics believe that the sacraments are the sources, or means, by which a person attains the condition of being in the right relationship and intimate union with God. Catholics refer to this condition as the "state of grace."

BAPTISM

Baptism is the ceremony in which a child or an adult convert is cleansed of sin to begin a new life with God. The name of the Trinity is invoked over the person being baptized. In the Orthodox churches the person being baptized is immersed in water and then marked with a cross with holy oil, while in the Catholic Church some water is poured over the person's head. In both cases these actions signify that the person is being cleansed of sin and that a new spiritual life is flowing into the baptized. These Christians believe that baptism also marks the beginning of a person's union with Christ and entry into the community of the church.

THE DIVINE LITURGY, OR MASS

This is the sacrament of Holy Eucharist, the central act of worship for both Catholics and Orthodox Christians.

CONFIRMATION

Often called chrismation in the Orthodox tradition, confirmation signifies the indwelling of the Holy Spirit upon the baptized person, just as the Spirit came upon the disciples on the first Pentecost. This sacrament strengthens a baptized person in the Christian faith and confers the grace that will enable that person to grow to spiritual adulthood. During this ceremony the baptized person is marked with the sign of the cross in chrism, or

A Catholic bishop conferring confirmation on a girl in Manchester, England. Receiving this sacrament is an important stage in the religious life of a young person and represents a coming of age. It is also a time of celebration for family, friends, and the church community.

holy oil (a sign of strength). In the Orthodox tradition this sacrament is conferred on the baptized person immediately following the sacrament of baptism. In the Catholic tradition the sacrament of confirmation represents the coming of age of the Catholic and so is not administered to infants. Another slight difference is that in the Catholic Church the bishop is the ordinary minister of the sacrament of confirmation. In the Orthodox and Eastern Catholic churches a priest is also permitted to confer this sacrament on those who are to receive it.

RECONCILIATION

Also called penance or confession, reconciliation is another sacrament that is shared by Catholic and Orthodox Christians. This is the sacrament of divine mercy, in which God's forgiving love is freely offered to any baptized person who seeks it, regardless of their sins. Both traditions believe that an individual's sins affect the whole church and that God's forgiveness is also offered through the church. The person who seeks God's forgiveness in this sacrament confesses his or her sins to a priest and expresses a sincere sorrow for having sinned and a willingness to refrain from future sin.

FORGIVENESS OF SINS

The role of the priest, as a representative of Christ, is to forgive the sinner. In the Catholic tradition this is done with the statement: "I absolve you from your sins in the name of the Father and of the Son and of the Holy Spirit." In the Eastern tradition the priest absolves him or her by saying: "May our Lord and God, Jesus Christ, through the grace and bounties of his love towards mankind, forgive you all your transgressions. And I, his unworthy priest, through the power given to me by Him, do forgive and absolve you from all your sins, in the name of the Father, and of the Son, and of the Holy Spirit."

MATRIMONY

Matrimony is the sacrament in which a man and a woman bind themselves to each other as husband and wife for life. Their Christian marriage is meant to express the reality of the unbreakable and intimate union between Jesus Christ and the church and between God and humanity. Catholic teaching does not recognize divorce or allow divorced persons to remarry, unless the original marriage has been annulled—declared by church law to have been invalid. Orthodox churches do not have annulments, but they do permit

A celebration of the sacrament of matrimony by a couple, witnessed by
their family and friends in a church in England.

divorce in certain cases and allow divorced persons to remarry. This is understood as a concession to human weakness in situations when the first marriage has definitively broken down and the divorced Christian seeks a second chance to live out a life of matrimonial communion. Eastern Catholic churches, like the Roman Catholic Church, forbid divorce, but they do grant annulments when the situation seems to warrant it.

HOLY ORDERS

This is the sacrament in which men chosen by the church are made deacons, priests, or bishops. The principal powers of the priesthood are those Christ gave his apostles, who were the first priests: to offer the holy Eucharist, forgive sins, administer the sacraments, and preach the Gospel. Since the Lateran Council of 1123 Catholic priests have not been permitted to marry. In the Orthodox churches parish priests are allowed to marry. However, a candidate may only marry prior to his ordination to the priesthood or diaconate, and not afterward. Only unmarried priests may become bishops in the Orthodox churches.

ANOINTING OF THE SICK

This sacrament gives the healing touch of Christ to an ill or suffering person. It is intended to bring strength to those who have been weakened by sickness, suffering, or old age. Both the Catholic and Orthodox churches confer this sacrament on their faithful.

CHURCH ORGANIZATION

At the present time church organization is the area that most divides the Catholic Church and the Orthodox churches. The major point of division is the role of the pope. Catholics believe that the pope is the representative of Christ on earth and thus the leader of the worldwide church. The Orthodox churches recognize that the pope, the bishop of Rome, has a special role in relation to all the churches of the world. However, they believe that this means he should be honored above all the other bishops, not that he can exercise direct authority over all the churches of the world. Because of this difference in understanding the role of the pope, the Orthodox churches and the Catholic Church are not in communion with each other. On the other hand Eastern Catholic churches are those churches that follow the Eastern traditions and liturgy but are in communion with the Roman Catholic Church. Eastern Catholic Christians pray for the pope during the Divine Liturgy and are part of the Catholic Church.

Despite these differences there are still many similarities between Catholics and Orthodox Christians with regard to church organization. The most important principle is that of apostolic succession. Both Catholic and Orthodox churches believe that the teaching of the apostles and the power that Christ conferred upon his apostles has been handed down in their churches through the succession of bishops that goes back to the earliest days of the church, the time when Christ's apostles lived. It is the belief of Catholics and Orthodox Christians that the hierarchy of the church is necessary to maintain the constant teaching of Christ and his apostles. Tradition plays a very important role in Catholic and Orthodox churches.

CATHOLIC CHURCH ORGANIZATION

The hierarchy of the Catholic Church has three levels: the pope, who is the bishop of Rome and the spiritual leader of the worldwide church; bishops, who are responsible for a diocese, or territorial district; and pastors, who are spiritual leaders of individual parishes. The pope appoints the bishops, who in turn appoint pastors.

AUTHORITY OF THE POPE

Catholics believe that the pope is infallible, or not able to err, in matters of faith and morals. This belief is based on the understanding that the church is guided

CARDINALS AND THE ROMAN CURIA

Assisting the pope in governing the church are two bodies, the College of Cardinals and the Roman Curia. The College of Cardinals is a group of Catholics, most often clergymen, appointed by the pope to serve as his advisers. They have the responsibility of electing a new pope when necessary. The Roman Curia serves as the pope's administrative arm. It consists of the secretariat of state, which assists the pope most directly in both governing the church and communicating with the rest of the Curia, and a number of other departments, each of which has a specific function.

by the presence of Christ and protected by the Holy Spirit from error. Catholics believe that this protection of the church from error takes place in the teachings of the pope when he speaks ex cathedra, or by virtue of his office. The pope does not have infallibility, or the inability to err, in connection with other aspects of church affairs, such as the running of a diocese or the books a Catholic publishing house might produce, but he does have absolute authority. He is considered the highest teacher, judge, and governing power in the church. The pope is assisted in the governance of the church by cardinals who belong to a body called the College of Cardinals. Many cardinals are archbishops of large diocese or regions, or they are heads of departments in the Roman Curia, the central administrative body of the Catholic Church.

CHURCH LAW AND CHURCH COURTS

The governing power of the Catholic Church over its members is twofold. It has a legislative, or lawmaking, role and a judicial role pertaining to the administration of church law. Church laws regulate the conduct of the church and its members. Church courts make decisions in matters pertaining to church law. The chief role of the church, however, is not to judge but to teach and exhort through its teaching. It is in few cases that the church deals with its members through any official legal system; generally it instructs through teaching and exhortation.

ORTHODOX CHURCH ORGANIZATION

The Orthodox churches are the major churches in Greece, Russia, eastern Europe, western Asia, and much of the Middle East. Individually they are usually called by their national names, such as the Greek Orthodox Church or the Russian Orthodox Church, but they are united by common beliefs and traditions. Most of the Orthodox churches in the United States are governed by the hierarchy of the country in which the particular church originated. For example, the Antiochian Orthodox Church is ultimately governed by the Antiochian Church in Syria, although it does have bishops in the United States. The three main religious orders within Orthodox churches are bishops, priests, and deacons although laity participate in the administration of their churches and the election of their clergy. Bishops are heads of major areas of a country, priests look after a specific parish, and deacons are assistants to the priests.

SELF-GOVERNING ORTHODOX CHURCHES

Among the self-governing churches, those of Constantinople, Alexandria, Antioch, and Jerusalem hold special places of honor in Orthodoxy for historical reasons. The greatest honor is given to the leader of the Church of Constantinople, who is called the ecumenical patriarch. His is a primacy of honor, and not of direct authority over all the Orthodox churches of the world. All the Orthodox churches pray for the ecumenical patriarch of Constantinople during the Divine Liturgy, just as Catholics express their communion with the pope by praying for him during Mass.

ORIENTAL ORTHODOX CHURCHES

There are also some Orthodox churches, the Oriental Orthodox churches, that do not recognize the primacy of honor of the patriarch of Constantinople. These are the churches, such as the allegedly Monophysite churches of the patriarchates of Alexandria and Antioch, that disagreed with the declaration of the Council of Chalcedon in 451. The Oriental Orthodox churches maintain good relations with the Eastern Orthodox churches and now generally agree that the doctrinal conflict was caused by a misunderstanding that was likely due to imprecise language and

The Orthodox Church of America

Early in the 20th century an attempt was made to unite all the Orthodox churches in the United States as a self-governing American church. This became the Orthodox Church of America, which was founded in 1970. However, this attempt did not succeed in uniting all the churches. Nevertheless many Orthodox Christians in America continue to work for a unified Orthodox American church.

ORTHODOX CLERGY

The three major orders of Orthodox clergy are the bishops, priests, and deacons. The two minor orders are the subdeacons and readers. Deacons, subdeacons, and readers assist the priest during religious services. Both the spiritual life and the administration of the churches are governed by the principle of shared responsibility between the clergy and the laity, or nonclergy. The laity often take part in the administration of their church and in the election of their clergy.

Members of the Ethiopian Orthodox Church during Eucharistic Liturgy in their church in the Holy Sepulchre, Jerusalem.

thus does not indicate a real difference of belief. According to this conciliatory interpretation of the ancient doctrinal conflict, all Orthodox churches hold that Christ is both God and man.

EASTERN CATHOLIC CHURCH ORGANIZATION

Eastern Catholic churches are united with Rome but their organizational structures parallel those of the various Eastern Orthodox churches. This is to be expected, since these Eastern Catholic churches have their origins in the same parts of the world as the Orthodox churches and have the same liturgy and traditions as their Orthodox counterparts. The main organizational difference, however, is that they elected to resume communion with the pope in Rome. This means that they both share the most holy religious services and accept the authority of the pope. These churches each have their own head, or patriarch. The internal affairs of each Eastern Catholic church are usually decided by the patriarch of that church and its bishops. The largest Eastern Catholic churches in the United States are the Melkite Church and the Maronite Church, which originated in the Middle East, and the Ukrainian and Ruthenian churches, which are Slavic in origin.

Whether in the Roman Catholic or in the Eastern Catholic churches, church organization is not considered to be exclusively a matter of administration and government. It is viewed as an ordering that is directed by the Holy Spirit for the maintenance of the church in the teachings of Jesus Christ. Such a spiritual view of organization is based on the words of Christ at the end of Matthew's Gospel: "And remember, I am with you always, to the end of the age." (Matthew 28:20)

CHAPTER 5

THE INFLUENCE OF THE CATHOLIC AND ORTHODOX CHURCHES

Throughout its history Christianity has had an impact in many areas of human life in the lands where it has been practiced. The extent of its influence has been greater or less in different countries at various times, but its influence was strongly felt in Europe during the Middle Ages, or as the period is sometimes called, the Age of Faith.

Comparatively, the influence of Catholicism, as with many forms of religion, has diminished in recent years, causing some Catholics to believe that today's world is too secular, or nonreligious. Yet even today the influence of the Catholic Church is strong. There is hardly a town in the United States that does not have at least one Catholic church. Many of the architecturally striking buildings in American and European cities are Catholic cathedrals. Catholic schools are recognized for the educational contributions they have made to American society. Moreover politicians and pollsters, those who canvas public opinion, are very aware of the power of the so-called Catholic vote.

Notre Dame Cathedral in Paris, France. A Christian basilica was first built here in the sixth century. Work on the current building began in 1163 and was completed in 1345.

In an early chapter of the Acts of the Apostles, Luke states that the followers of Christ continued to gather in Jerusalem and that they shared their belongings with one another. "They would sell their possessions and goods and distribute the proceeds to all, as any had need." (Acts 2:45) During the earliest days of the church Christians must not have stood out that much from other Jews who followed a particular teacher. They went to the synagogue and dressed like the other Jews. They celebrated the Sabbath and religious feasts, even though they were beginning to give them new Christian meanings or interpretations.

IMITATING GOD'S LOVE

As the church spread among the Greek and other non-Jewish communities, Christ's followers were also not noticeably different from the rest of their countrymen. Christians were not identified by peculiar customs or a particular language that set them apart from their neighbors. Rather Christ's followers were found among non-Christians in various countries, and they lived life very much as it was lived by other citizens. Yet Christians throughout the ages have tried to point out what makes them different from other people. Their special calling is to imitate God's love.

Love, as Christians envision it, cannot be something true Christians engage in just on Sundays and ignore or forget about during the rest of the week. Nor is it measured in terms of loving someone because he or she returns that love. According to Christians God's love for people is not conditional on their reciprocal love. He loves us simply, unreservedly, and unconditionally. That is the model of love God sets for his people. Christians see the life and death of God in Jesus Christ as

FIRST LETTER OF SAINT JOHN

Many religions demand that their followers love God with all their heart and soul and love their neighbors as they love themselves. The special approach of Christian love is stated in the First Letter of Saint John. In this way the love of God was revealed to us:

God sent his only Son into the world so that we might have life through him. In this is love: not that we have loved God, but that he loved us and sent his Son as expiation for our sins. Beloved, since God has so loved us, we also must love one another.

—1 John 4:9–11

inaugurating a new kingdom in which the ethics of unconditional love permeate all existence.

SUNDAY EUCHARIST

The celebration of the Sunday Eucharist (sometimes called the "love feast" in the early church) is considered an exemplary model of the communion that all people are meant to experience not only with God but also with each other. One of the Eastern fathers of the church, Saint John Chrysostom (ca. 347–407), insisted that just as all Christians participate equally in the Eucharist of Christ, they should work for the equal sharing of all worldly goods. In a similar spirit the Catholic philosopher Blaise Pascal (1623–62) is reported to have invited poor people into his house for a meal when he was too sick to attend the Eucharist in church.

Family and friends receive the Eucharist from the priest at the Immaculate Conception Catholic Church in Hialeah, Florida, where they have gathered for a special mass on the day of a teen girl's Quince Años, a traditional Hispanic coming-of-age celebration of a girl's 15th birthday.

Greek Orthodox children leading a Palm Sunday procession on the island of Syros, Greece. Palm Sunday marks the sixth and last Sunday of Lent and the beginning of Holy Week leading up to Easter Sunday.

RELIGIOUS PRACTICE

In the United States today Catholics generally practice their religion without much fanfare. They practice their faith in the atmosphere of their families, or in church on Sunday. In the Eastern Catholic tradition the customary Lenten fast is to abstain from meat and dairy products for the entire 40 days of Lent, though sometimes modifications of this tradition are allowed. Special Lenten services in the Eastern Rite are observed two or three times a week and every day during the climactic Holy Week that extends from Palm Sunday to Easter Sunday. Religious services are also held on important Catholic feast days, such as Easter and Christmas. Most Catholics, however, live their visible lives in the same way as other citizens. They wear no special clothing and rarely follow any special dietary regulations. Some children may attend parochial, or church-run, schools, but many also attend public schools. For the most part there is no significant difference between the Catholic population and the general population in the life they live.

COMMUNITIES COMMITTED TO GOD

A few Catholic communities, because of their particular dedication to the Gospel teachings, do live quite differently from their neighbors. Catholic priests, monks, and nuns at times have worn distinctive dress within and outside their religious houses. These distinctive garments were meant to set them apart as a group whose members were in a special way committed to dedicating their lives to God. Unlike these special groups, however, most Christians dress in the various styles of the times, in no way reflecting their religious beliefs.

EDUCATION

Christ's first apostles were not scholars. They were fishermen. Christ did not suggest that scholars were particularly qualified to preach the Gospel.

Christian scholars such as Tertullian (ca. 160–ca. 225), himself a highly educated person, wished to employ his intellectual talents in the service of the simplicity of the Gospel and was afraid that the worldly wisdom of his time would undermine Christian teachings. For example, the schools of the classical world of Greece and Rome used for their basic texts the works of writers such as Homer and Virgil, with their tales of vengeful gods and stories of heroes who seemed to be centered upon their own achievements. There were in fact many reasons for Christians to become anti-intellectual, since the early Greek and Roman intellectual worlds, from a Christian perspective, offered such poor examples to follow.

Many resisted this temptation, however. Justin Martyr (ca. 100–ca. 165) realized that his search for life's meaning through the study of pagan classics was not satisfying. He was looking for something more than these classics provided, and so he turned to the study of the Gospels.

UNDERSTANDING AND EXPLORING THE GOSPELS

Other Christians found the teachings of the Gospels to be misunderstood or misrepresented by opponents. They realized that they needed skills in logic and rhetoric to disprove them. Thus Christians saw the need for studying the traditional subjects of the seven liberal arts that the ancient Greeks and Romans studied—grammar, rhetoric, dialectic, arithmetic, geometry, music, and astronomy—to defend and explain the teachings of the Gospels. Saint Augustine, in his work *On Christian Teaching*, argued strongly that these studies were key to understanding, explaining, and defending the biblical writings.

A CHRISTIAN LANGUAGE

It was not, however, a matter of simply learning the same subjects as were taught in the non-Christian schools. There was the need to develop the kind of learning that would be properly Christian. This task involved the development of a Christian language. Saint Clement of Alexandria employed a famous image to illustrate this effort: the new song of the divine Word demanded new words. There were no existing words capable of describing the Christian God who is three persons. Words like *Trinity* or *Triune God* had to be coined by Christians to express the special character of their God.

The same was true of Jesus Christ, that is, God the Son who took on human flesh. To express the reality of Christ, their Redeemer, Christians had to invent the word *Savior*. When Christians invented words like *Savior* non-Christian grammarians must have ridiculed their new word. Saint Augustine, in one of his sermons, tells his audience not to worry about the laughter of the grammarians. Christians should rather focus on how true the new expression is. Before the coming of Christ, he notes, there was no Savior, so people who were not Christians did not have a word for a reality that did not exist for them.

Often, however, there were words available, but Christians had to give them new meanings. There was a Greek word *catechumenus,* which meant "learner." The Christians gave it a new meaning: "someone who is learning about the Christian faith."

The word *pagan* was a military term that referred to those who were civilians and not soldiers. For Christians, a pagan was a person who was not a soldier of Christ. Very many words for Christians had to take on new meanings or had to be invented. Christian education had many challenges to face, and it took a great deal of effort to develop Christian language and meaning within non-Christian schools. Eventually Christians developed their own schools.

CHRISTIAN SCHOOLS

Schools attached to monasteries and cathedrals were built to educate people who did not intend to pursue church positions. As more towns were established and more cathedrals were built, these schools increased in number throughout Europe, especially in France. Many of the major universities of Europe developed from such schools. The Catholic Church, as part of its own reform movement in the 16th and 17th centuries, also expanded its educational activities. Schools were established for Catholic children in which they were taught in their own languages.

ORTHODOX SCHOLARSHIP

In the Orthodox Christian tradition scholarship was central, as the Orthodox churches were heirs to the philosophical wisdom and insights of the greatest thinkers of antiquity. Indeed, in some Orthodox churches paintings will be found of philosophers such as Plato and Aristotle, who are seen as forebears of Christian wisdom. Eastern theologians such as Saints Basil the Great (ca. 329–79), Gregory of Nyssa (ca. 330–ca. 395), and Gregory Nazianzen (ca. 329–90) were highly versed in the philosophical and general knowledge of their time and brought Christianity into the wider world of thinking. Saint Basil is especially well known for his essay written to adolescents encouraging them to read the Greek classics, since Christians cannot afford to be unlettered. For another Eastern Christian theologian, Saint Maximos the Confessor (ca. 580–622), knowledge, not just moral discipline, was an important step in the Christian's progress in the spiritual life. In modern times we can again point to the example of the popular Russian priest Father Alexander Men (1935–90), who saw all human culture as a valuable witness to humanity's search for God, a search fulfilled in the divine-human person of Jesus Christ.

CATHOLIC EDUCATION IN AMERICA

Most immigrants who came to the Americas from Europe set up the kinds of schools they had known in their homelands. Saint Elizabeth Bayley Seton (1774–1821), founder of the American Sisters of Charity, was the architect of the parochial school system in the United States. She received her inspiration from the training established in France by Louise de Marillac (1591–1660), the cofounder of the Sisters of Charity. Under such inspiration Catholics established and supported their own schools. Most of these were elementary schools where reading, writing, and religion were taught. Later secondary schools and even small colleges were founded by churches, primarily to train young men for the ministry. By the 20th century many of these colleges had developed into large and respected universities.

ART AND ARCHITECTURE

Although the Christian church did not continue many of the ritual laws of the Jewish people, it did hold to the Ten Commandments. The first commandment prohibits the making of images of anything in heaven or on earth that could serve as an idol. This prohibition made the early Christians hesitant to create any images at all. The earliest works of Christian art began appearing in the third century in the form of mural paintings in burial chambers such as the Roman catacombs. The subjects of these paintings included Christ's early miracle of the multiplication of the loaves and fishes and scenes based on other biblical stories.

The Church of Hagia Sophia in Istanbul, Turkey. The church was built between 532 and 537 by the emperor Justinian. The first church on this site was built by the emperor Constantine, the first Christian emperor of Rome, when he moved the capital of the Empire from Rome to Byzantium in 330.

MOSAICS, PAINTINGS, AND MANUSCRIPTS

As the church came out of hiding in the fourth century, after years of persecution, works of Christian art began to appear. This can be seen in the beautiful mosaics that survive in the Church of San Vitale of Ravenna, Italy, or in the Cathedral of Monreale in Sicily, or in the illuminations (special ornamental illustrations) found in early manuscripts of the Vatican library. Before monarchs, lords, and wealthy merchants began to patronize artists during the Renaissance almost all art was religious art, commis-

A Russian icon of Mary, the Mother of God, holding Jesus, the Son of God. The golden halo, a circular ring of light around their heads, is used in Christian religious art to denote the light of grace bestowed by God.

sioned by and for the church. By the 500s a distinct style of art and architecture had developed in the Byzantine Empire. In the domed churches of Byzantium, tapestries, mosaics, paintings, and murals recounting the life of Christ and the careers of saints and martyrs adorned every surface. This tradition continues to this day in all Orthodox churches.

THE MIDDLE AGES

The Middle Ages in Europe were a period of deep religious faith. The church became the period's most influential patron of the arts, building churches and monasteries, decorating them with paintings, and filling them with altars, candelabra, and screens made of wood or iron. The frescoes, or paintings on fresh plaster, of the 14th-century Italian painter Giotto (ca. 1266–1337) and the stained glass of Chartres Cathedral in France, for example, are visible reminders of this age of glory for Christian art.

MAKING ICONS

The Medieval and Renaissance periods also saw the flourishing of the great Byzantine tradition of making icons. From this period we have two of the most beloved icons in the Orthodox tradition. One of these is *The Vladimir Madonna,* also known as *The Mother of Loving Kindness,* which depicts a tender embrace between the Mother of God—to use the Orthodox description of Mary—and the child Jesus. It was painted in the 12th century and presented as a gift honoring Prince Vladimir of Russia (ca. 956–1015) by the patriarch of Constantinople. The other is known as *The Old Testament Trinity* or *The Hospitality of Abraham and Sarah,* which presents the angels who visit Abraham and Sarah, according to the Old Testament account, as a symbol of the Triune God. The icon was painted by one of the great Byzantine Russian painters, Andrei Rublev (ca. 1360–1430) in the 15th century.

INSPIRING REVERENCE

Architects in the early part of the Middle Ages built churches modeled after Rome's great buildings. This Romanesque archi-

RENAISSANCE ART

Even though much art during the Renaissance—the 15th- and 16th-centuries revival of Greek and Roman artistic forms—began to be sponsored by non-church patrons, and artists were increasingly creating paintings and sculptures for private enjoyment, some of the greatest works of religious art were created during this period. Pope Julius II (1503–13) made Rome an important artistic center. Among the works of art he commissioned was the painting of the ceiling of the Sistine Chapel in the Vatican by Michelangelo (1475–1564). Other famous artists of the time included Raphael (1483–1520), renowned for *The Marriage of the Virgin* and *The Transfiguration,* and Leonardo da Vinci (1452–1519), best known for *The Last Supper.*

The ceiling of the Sistine Chapel in the Vatican,
painted by Michelangelo.

tecture, however, took on fresh, creative forms. The more definitively Christian form of architecture is found later in the Middle Ages with the development of Gothic cathedrals, such as the Cathedral of Notre Dame in France or Cologne Cathedral in Germany, with arches and towers that seem to soar to heaven. These cathedrals were intended to inspire a mood of reverence among worshippers, lifting their hearts to the heavens above. The invention of supports for the soaring walls of the cathedral freed them for windows. Magnificent stained-glass windows became the principal form of internal decoration in these cathedrals. As they knelt before richly carved altars, surrounded by beautiful images, bathed in colored light that had filtered through the stained-glass windows, medieval worshippers must have felt both awed and uplifted. During the 15th and 16th centuries there was a revival of art using Greek and Roman artistic forms, which became known as the Renaissance period. It was during this time that many great works of religious art were commissioned by nonreligious as well as religious patrons.

TRADITION OF EASTERN ART

During the Protestant Reformation, which began in 1517 and transformed the face of Europe and Christianity over the next 150 years, the Catholic Church attempted at times to counter the charges of immorality and idolatry that were launched by the reformers. Church painting was more strictly regulated. Pope Pius V (1566–72) went so far as to order clothing added to the figures Michelangelo had painted in the Sistine Chapel.

However, the art and architecture of Orthodox Christendom were relatively unaffected by these movements of Reformation and Counter-Reformation. Orthodox churches continued to be built in the classic Byzantine style. They also were adorned with icons, especially on the iconostasis, or screen that stands between the congregation and the sanctuary with its altar.

Eastern Catholics likewise continued these architectural practices. For them, as well as for the Orthodox, such features were not simply ornamental but aided their understanding of the

The haunting melancholy chant that commemorates the crucifixion of Christ exemplifies the style of sung Byzantine liturgy:

Today he who hung the earth upon the waters is hung upon a tree
The King of the angels is adorned with a crown of thorns
He who wraps the heavens with clouds is wrapped with the purple of mockery
He who set Adam free . . . receives blows upon his face
The Bridegroom of the Church is pierced through with nails
The Son of the Virgin is stabbed with a spear
We venerate your Passion, O Christ, Show us also your glorious Resurrection.

Plainsong

Plainsong, a simple form of vocal music, was so called because a soloist or choir sang the melody without instrumental accompaniment or harmony. Plainsong developed gradually from early Jewish religious music, and much of it was set to the words of the Psalms, lyrical poems from the Old Testament. The most important type of plainsong was Gregorian chant, developed in the time of Pope Gregory I (590–604).

church as a concrete manifestation of the kingdom of God and the communion of saints.

MUSIC

Christianity played an important part in the early growth of classical music. However, this was not the first influence Christianity had on music. The oldest known Christian form of music was plainsong, a simple form of vocal music that was used in early Catholic Church services.

BYZANTINE LITURGY

For the Orthodox Church music began to play an increasing role in the liturgy during the period of the Byzantine Empire, from about the fourth to the 15th century. About the end of the fifth century Romanus (490–556), a Greek monk, composed the words and music of hymns that still form part of the Byzantine liturgy. Musical expression has always been a prominent feature of the Orthodox Christian tradition. To this day the Byzantine liturgy is for the most part sung rather than recited. Orthodox Christians give great honor to the early poet-theologians who penned many of the traditional hymns. These hymns emphasize central aspects of the Christian faith.

GREEK AND RUSSIAN STYLES

For the most part in the Orthodox tradition the chants in the sung liturgy normally have no instrumental accompaniment.

Orthodox Christians hold that the most fitting instrument to use in liturgical worship is the human voice, since Christians believe that the human being was created in the image of God. A slight exception to this rule is the use of cymbals in the Coptic (Egyptian) tradition. Of the two main styles of Orthodox Christian music, the Greek and the Russian, the former tends to be simpler and more rhythmic, while the latter is more elaborate and makes greater use of harmony. The Russian style reached a high point of harmonic complexity and richness in the High Renaissance and Baroque periods. In more recent times some of the great Russian composers have also composed liturgical works.

WESTERN MUSICAL DEVELOPMENT

In the Western tradition an Italian Benedictine monk named Guido d'Arezzo (ca. 995–ca. 1049) revolutionized the teaching of music during the 11th century. He introduced the four-line staff and is credited with establishing the first six notes of the scale. These achievements made the teaching of music much easier. Another great musical innovation of the 11th century was polyphony—the putting together of two or more voices harmoniously. In the 1300s, the French composer Guillaume de Machaut (1300–77) wrote the first polyphonic Catholic Mass.

Many forms of classical music were created for church services. Most choral music in particular has been written for religious ceremonies. The principal form of such choral music is the mass, a series of pieces composed for a Catholic worship service. The earliest masses were written for small, unaccompanied choruses. Only later did polyphonic masses develop, at times accompanied by instruments. The requiem, which is a special mass composed for funerals, also frequently involves choral singing. Requiems

RUSSIAN CHORAL MUSIC

Since the 19th century liturgical and devotional music has been composed by some of the great Russian composers. High points within this tradition include the setting to music of the Liturgy of Saint John Chrysostom by Pyotr Tchaikovsky (1840–93), as well as the Great Vespers of Sergey Rachmaninoff (1873–1943). Other secular composers who composed Byzantine choral music are Pavel Chesnokov (1877–1944), Dmitry Bortnyansky (1751–1825), and Igor Stravinsky (1882–1971). Stravinsky is well known in the West for his *Firebird Suite* and *The Rite of Spring*, but he is equally well known in Slavic lands for his musical rendering of the Our Father and for other liturgical music.

Sister Lucia Morales leading hymns during a bilingual Maundy Thursday Mass in Spanish and English at Saint Alexius Catholic Church in Beardstown, Illinois.

have been written by such composers as Wolfgang Amadeus Mozart (1756–91), Louis-Hector Berlioz (1803–69), and Giuseppe Verdi (1813–1901).

A hymn is a song of praise, and most hymns glorify God. Since biblical times Jews have used the Psalms of the Old Testament in their services. Until the 1500s most Christian hymns were sung in Latin. In recent years many of these Latin hymns have been rewritten in vernacular, or local language, forms. They have also been joined by a completely new collection of hymns supported by guitars. These hymns have very much been developed to encourage a more active musical participation by the whole community of worshippers.

LITERATURE

Early Christian authors such as Tertullian (ca. 160–ca. 225), Saint John Chrysostom (ca. 347–407), and Saint Augustine (354–430), are widely considered by classical scholars to be among the finest stylists of classical Greek and Latin respectively. In the West it was as the language of the church—no longer of the Roman Empire—that Latin was to remain alive and vigorous up to the end of the Middle Ages.

MONASTERY RECORDS AND LIBRARIES

After the fall of Rome many European monasteries were founded that preserved Christianity and classical learning. Monastery libraries contained not only Bibles, biblical commentaries, and liturgical books, but also the classics of ancient Greece and Rome that otherwise would have been lost forever. Monasteries also fostered the emergence of literature in the vernacular, as opposed to Latin. These libraries with their faithful copies of texts provided the raw materials that later would form the basis of Charlemagne's (ca. 742–814) educational reforms.

A wealth of literature was produced from the beginning of the fifth to the 17th century in Europe, and many of the most admired works were written by Catholic authors. Although some of these works, such as the records of monasteries compiled by Christian monks during the Middle Ages, were merely histories of monastic foundations, others, such as the *Ecclesiastical History of the English Nation* written by a British monk called the Venerable Bede (673–735), were masterpieces. Bede wrote many works on science, grammar, history, and theology.

LITERATURE OF THE EASTERN TRADITION

In the Christian East the same period saw the flourishing of literature that dealt with progress in the spiritual life. Among the most important writers of the period were Saint John Climacus (525–606), whose *Ladder of Divine Ascent* is considered a classic of Orthodox spirituality, and Saint

The *Canterbury Tales*

One of the most celebrated classics of early English literature, Geoffrey Chaucer's (ca. 1340–1400) *Canterbury Tales* came out of the medieval tradition of pilgrimages, journeys made by people of diverse backgrounds to sacred places. Chaucer's tales relate the adventures of a group of pilgrims on their way to the shrine in Canterbury of the murdered archbishop Thomas à Becket.

Symeon the New Theologian (949–1022), whose experiences of God as "divine fire" are based on the scene of Jesus's transfiguration before his disciples in the Gospel accounts.

In the 19th century the Orthodox Christian culture of Russia gave rise to some of the most monumental classics of modern literature. Great Russian authors such as Fyodor Dostoyevsky (1821–81) and Leo Tolstoy (1828–1910) were preoccupied with religious questions. Their major works deal directly with religious themes and treat them in a way that is explicitly Christian.

MODERN CATHOLIC LITERATURE

Catholic literature has continued to develop in the modern and contemporary period and has done so in many forms. Theological and philosophical themes have been elaborated in the writings of Jacques Maritain (1882–1973), Étienne Gilson (1884–1978), Pierre Teilhard de Chardin (1881–1955), and Gabriel Marcel (1889–1973). The novels of Graham Greene (1904–91) have often wrestled with the moral dilemmas facing Catholics in the contemporary world, and the works of Flannery O'Connor (1925–64) have often treated themes challenging Catholics and many other religious people today. Other writers, such as Thomas Keneally and David Lodge (both born in 1935), grapple with the issues of being Catholics in contemporary society from the angle of those whose heritage is Catholic but who now move in a wider circle of influences.

THEATER

Christianity's influence on the theater (and circus) was at first negative. In Rome and Constantinople many forms of theater were popular—tragedy, comedy, farce, and pantomime. Circuses in Rome were built with a crescent-shaped tiered seating area facing an open performance area. As well as being the site of various sports competitions, chariot races and staged battles, the circus was also one of the places where many Christians had been martyred, by being hunted down or crucified for public entertainment. Because the organ was originally a musical instrument designed for use in the circus, it was for centuries considered a deeply inappropriate instrument for church music—and is still viewed with suspicion by the Orthodox Church. Most of the

The remains of the Circus Maximus (Great Circus) in Rome. Although little is now left of the site, at one time up to 250,000 Romans came to watch the events here. This was one of the sites in Rome where many early Christians were martyred for public entertainment.

theater performances were considered offensive to the early Christians, and as Christianity grew more powerful the theater declined. In the 400s actors were excommunicated or denied participation in church functions, and Roman theater came to an end not long afterward. The last known theatrical performance in ancient Rome was in 533.

At the same time Christian worship itself increasingly acquired a dramatic form. This development began in the Christian East as the Byzantine liturgy admitted a number of processions within the liturgy. Increasingly the Eucharistic Liturgy came to be interpreted as a drama that reenacted the life and death of Jesus. Byzantine hymns also developed a more dramatic form, consisting of dialogues between various figures in the Gospel narrative. A Christmas hymn, for example, would consist of a chanted conversation among Mary, Joseph, the angels, and the shepherds. The Passion of Christ often was sung by a large cast joined by the surrounding mob.

CHRISTIAN PLAYS

The rebirth of drama in the Roman Catholic Church began in the 900s when priests and choirboys began to act out short plays as part of the worship service, especially in the church's attempt to make the Gospels come alive. A large body of plays grew up around the Resurrection, the Christmas story, and other biblical events. The language of these plays was the language of the church: Latin.

MYSTERY PLAYS

In the 1300s plays moved outdoors and began to be produced and acted by nonreligious groups such as the craft or trade organizations called guilds. The plays came to be called mystery plays from another name for these guilds: masteries or mysteries.

Mystery plays were staged outdoors on large carts called pageant wagons. A wagon was drawn through a town to various places where spectators stood in the street or watched from nearby houses. The actors were townspeople, most of whom belonged to the guilds that produced the plays. Mystery plays were presented in cycles of several related dramas over a period of one or two days. Each guild in a town was responsible for one episode or play. The play was in the local language.

MIRACLE PLAYS

Miracle plays, which developed out of mystery plays, were also popular during the Middle Ages. Like mystery plays they were presented initially as part of Catholic church services but lost the approval of the church. After being driven out of the churches and into the streets, miracle plays were performed by trade guild members on feast days. Miracle plays dramatized events from the life of the Virgin Mary or the lives of saints. The action of most of these plays reached a climax in a miracle performed by a saint—which gave these plays their name.

MORALITY PLAYS

Another form of medieval drama, the morality play, was first produced in England in the 1400s. Like the mystery and the miracle play, the morality play developed from religious pageants. Its purpose was to teach a lesson or to show the eternal struggle between good and evil for control of human beings. The morality play became more fully developed than other types of medieval drama, growing from a fairly simple religious play to a secular entertainment performed by professional companies of actors. While morality plays were primarily serious, the characters who represented evil were usually treated in a comical way to make the play more entertaining to the audience. The clowns and fools in the plays of William Shakespeare (1564–1616), such as Bottom in *A Midsummer Night's Dream* and Dogberry in *Much Ado About Nothing*, developed out

SPANISH RELIGIOUS DRAMA

In Spain during the Middle Ages drama became an important vehicle for religious teaching. Spanish religious plays combined elements of the mystery play and the morality play. Human and supernatural characters mingled with symbolic figures, such as Grace, Pleasure, and Sin. Dramatists borrowed their stories from both secular and religious sources, adapting them to uphold church teachings. Like the English mystery plays the Spanish plays were performed outdoors on wagons.

of the comic characters in morality plays. Everyman, a favorite morality play of the 1500s, is still performed annually at a music and drama festival in Salzburg, Austria.

EUROPEAN PASSION PLAYS

During the late Middle Ages European townspeople and villagers often staged passion plays. These were performances that depicted the suffering, crucifixion, and death of Jesus Christ. By taking part in a passion play, townspeople also participated in the

drama of Christ's last days on earth. The passion play tradition continues to the present in towns in southern Germany, western Austria, and Switzerland. The most famous one is held every 10 years in the Bavarian town of Oberammergau.

MODERN PRODUCTIONS

In modern times biblical themes and stories continue to be used as material in the creation of theatrical productions and movies. One contemporary example is *The Passion of the Christ* directed by Mel Gibson, which drew a lot of attention. Another example is a series of films, *The Decalogue,* based on the biblical Ten Commandments, by acclaimed Polish director Krzysztof Kieslowski (1941–96). In this collection of films dramatic situations are created in modern settings in ways that explore the themes of the Ten Commandments. Anyone who is familiar with biblical lore will find that in these films, and in works of music, art, and literature throughout the course of Western civilization, there are many explicit references to the resources of the Christian tradition.

People carry a wooden cross into the Holy Sepulchre in Jerusalem at Easter to reenact Christ's last journey through the streets on the way to his crucifixion at Calvary.

CHAPTER 6

CATHOLICISM AND ORTHODOX CHRISTIANITY FACING NEW CHALLENGES

Even a brief study of the history of Christianity would make a person aware of the truth of Christ's words: "My kingdom is not of this world." (John 18:36) For Catholics and Orthodox Christians the peace promised by Christ is found only in the kingdom of heaven. In this earthly life, believers sense themselves as pilgrims on a journey to the promised land. In this life they expect challenges, difficulties, sin, weakness, misunderstanding, rejection, persecution, and even death.

Yet the faith and hope of Catholics and Orthodox Christians are anchored in the resurrection of Christ that followed his sufferings and death. They believe, despite all appearances to the contrary, in the mysterious providence of God. They also believe that God works through them as his instruments in establishing a foretaste of his heavenly kingdom here on earth. They realize that their calling from God is to face the challenges of life and to do so as they imagine Christ would.

Pope Benedict XVI, right, is greeted by Ecumenical Orthodox Patriarch Bartholomew I as he arrives at Istanbul's St. George's Church for a service in November 2006.

Pope John Paul II, after reigning for 26 years as pope, died on April 2, 2005. For younger Catholics he was the only pope they had ever known. He had been a charismatic leader who traveled to all parts of the world, urging his flock to follow the Gospel teachings. In a special way, he had an apostolate to young believers, frequently attending their congresses throughout the world. In an attempt to preserve the unity of his flock he had established a strong centralized authority and proclaimed the strength of traditional Catholic moral habits and teachings. He had also reached out to Orthodox Christians and to members of other religious communities.

ELECTION OF A NEW POPE

On April 19, 2005, Joseph Cardinal Ratzinger was elected to succeed Pope John Paul. He took the name Benedict XVI. Cardinal Ratzinger had for much of his priestly life been a professor of philosophy and theology, a scholar in the history of Christian teachings, and the author of many books. He was appointed by Pope John Paul II to lead the revision of *The Catechism of the Catholic Church,* a work published in 1992. Earlier, in 1981, he was nominated by his predecessor as prefect of the Congregation for the Doctrine of the Faith, an office that required him to be the guardian of the Catholic faith.

"SERVANT OF THE SERVANTS OF GOD"

As pope, Benedict XVI's office has further requirements. Gregory the Great viewed the pope as "the servant of the servants of God." Others have seen the parable of the Good Shepherd as the guide for bishops and popes. Some cardinals have suggested that Cardinal Ratzinger was elected to succeed Pope John Paul II because the 115 cardinal electors desired to find someone most like Pope John Paul.

Benedict has proved to be a surprise to many because he has opened up the Papacy to new ideas and has become a powerful force for reflection on contemporary society and Catholicism.

His strong emphasis on ecology, his opposition to the war in Iraq, his moving first encyclical on the meaning of love—which some have described as more like a poem than a papal missive—have all shown him to be someone willing to tackle deep issues profoundly.

ECUMENICAL PATRIARCH OF CONSTANTINOPLE

One of the most important figures in the contemporary Orthodox world is the ecumenical patriarch of Constantinople, Bartholomew. Elected to the post in 1991, he has sought to unite the Orthodox world after the collapse of Communism and in 1993 was able, as the "First Among Equals," to call a meeting of all the heads of all the Orthodox churches. At these meetings theological and social issues were fully explored and among these was the environment. Over the last few decades the ecumenical patriarch has taken a lead in addressing the environment, earning him-

The ecumenical patriarch of Constantinople, Bartholomew, with Maha Ghosananda, a Buddhist teacher and peace campaigner, and Sikh and Jewish representatives at a multifaith religion and environment conference in Atami, Japan, 1995.

self the title "the green patriarch." He has also sought to strengthen the links with the Catholic Church as well as with other major Christian traditions.

ECUMENISM

Among the traditional marks or characteristics of the church is unity. The Nicene Creed, accepted by the Catholic and Orthodox churches, expresses the attributes of the church in these terms: "I believe in the one, holy, catholic, and apostolic Church." The split, or schism, between the Catholic and Orthodox churches is considered a scandal against the church's attribute of unity by many believers. This gulf between Catholics and the Orthodox churches has been multiplied, and the scandal intensified, by the many divisions of Protestant Christianity following their separation from the Catholic Church in the 16th century.

UNITY OF ALL CHRISTIANS

Efforts have been made to heal the rifts between divided Christians since the time of the splits, but these efforts have intensified in the 20th century. The efforts promoting this movement have been given the name *ecumenical* (meaning "worldwide" or "all the inhabited world"). The Catholic Church has become very active in the ecumenical movement since the time of the Second Vatican Council (1962–65). At this worldwide council Catholic Church leaders passed a Decree on Ecumenism that pledged the church to work for the unity of all Christianity and encouraged Catholics to take part in this ecumenical effort. The decree also permitted Catholics to join non-Catholics in common prayer, with the permission of the local bishops.

Pope Benedict XVI holds a mass with cardinals and some 57,000 people at Yankee Stadium in New York in April 2008.

DIALOGUE WITH CHURCHES

These efforts continue today. On May 8, 2005, for instance, less than a month after his election, Benedict XVI sent greetings and prayers to the national synod of the Reformed Church of France. On their side many Protestant churches have made an effort on the international level to promote dialogue and some form of unity through the World Council of Churches that was formed in Amsterdam, the Netherlands, in 1948. This is a major forum for the various Christian churches to dialogue with one another with the goal of seeking reunification. The Catholic Church did not become a member of this council, preferring to carry out individual dialogues with particular churches. Most Orthodox churches have chosen to join the World Council. The Orthodox play a role within the World Council of Churches, though there are times when the Orthodox theological perspective is at variance with the more liberal Protestant theology of the council.

Catholics and Orthodox Christians recognize the great similarities between their traditions, their teachings, and their liturgies. Yet despite these many similarities attempts at agreement are difficult to achieve. In 1965 the Catholic Church took a step toward ending the divisions between itself and the Orthodox churches. On December 7 of that year Pope Paul VI (1963–78) removed the sentence of excommunication, or exclusion from the rites of the church, that was placed on the patriarch of Constantinople in 1054. The patriarch of Constantinople in turn removed a sentence of excommunication that the 11th-century patriarch had passed against a group of papal delegates.

A decree of the Second Vatican Council also reaffirmed the equality of the rites of the Eastern and Western churches. It recognized that the Orthodox churches have valid sacraments and set forth circumstances under which Catholics and Orthodox Christians could participate together in the sacraments and worship. Although the Catholic Church allows Orthodox Christians under certain circumstances to participate in the Eucharistic Liturgy of the Catholic Church, the Orthodox churches do not adopt the same policy toward Catholics. They judged that participation in each other's sacraments is a sign of unity and should not be engaged in before this unity is fully realized.

Pope John Paul II was elected to the papacy in October 1978. His pontificate, lasting nearly 27 years, was one of the longest in the history of the Catholic Church. He took part in the Second Vatican Council and worked toward unification with the Orthodox churches.

THE ROLE OF THE PAPACY

Today it is generally agreed that the major obstacle to the reunification of the Catholic and Orthodox churches is their different understandings of the role of the papacy. Catholics believe that the pope is the center of unity for the worldwide church and has the authority to rule over any part of the universal church. They also believe that the pope has been granted the gift of speaking infallibly, or is incapable of error, in matters of faith and doctrine, so that the church may be guarded from serious error and departure from the Gospel message.

The Orthodox, on the other hand, believe that the pope is the first among bishops in the world and has a moral authority of honor that should be respected among all the world's churches. However they do not agree that the pope should directly govern all the churches of the world. The Orthodox also believe that the infallible teaching of the church must be agreed upon in a universal gathering of bishops and not merely through the teaching of the pope. Pope John Paul II had made it a priority of his pontificate to seek reunification with the Orthodox churches. In an important encyclical letter, *Ut Unum Sint* (Latin for "That all may be one"), he suggested that the Catholic Church is open to dialogue on the issue of the role of the papacy in order to arrive at a common understanding with the Orthodox churches.

HEALING AN ANCIENT DIVIDE

Pope John Paul II committed himself seriously to pursuing the path to unity and his successor, Benedict XVI, has given strong signs early in his pontificate that he intends to follow the same road. His first visit outside of Rome was to Bari, the coastal city in Italy that is a sacred site for Orthodox Christians because the bones of a respected patron, Saint Nicholas, are there. At the church of Saint Nicholas the pope declared: "Precisely here in Bari . . . land of meeting and dialogue with our Christian brothers of the East, I would like to confirm my wish to assume as a fundamental commitment to work with all my energies on the reconstitution of the full and visible unity of all the followers of Christ."

On the Orthodox side the initiatives to heal this ancient divide came from the ecumenical patriarchate in Constantinople. In particular the current ecumenical patriarch of Constantinople, Bartholomew, has invited the pope to visit and has renewed theological dialogue with the Catholic Church.

The ecumenical patriarch has also healed a 1,500-year schism between the Orthodox churches and the Monophysite churches such as the Coptic, Ethiopian, and Armenian churches. This major healing of such an ancient division has been remarkable and is a sign of the shift in perceptions between the Orthodox and the Oriental Orthodox. While Catholic-Orthodox reunion is still a long way off, the Orthodox-Oriental resolution indicates that reconciliation can be achieved. It is a remarkable achievement of the churches.

INTERRELIGIOUS DIALOGUE

The attempts of Catholic and Orthodox Christians to promote efforts at unity between themselves and with other Christian denominations continues to be one of the major challenges for Christians today. Further, these same or similar efforts need to be extended, since they are necessary as well in regard to Jews and Muslims, who share in major ways the same biblical tradition. Increasingly both Catholic and Orthodox leaders are playing a key role in working with other faiths on issues such as the environment, health, and aspects of religious fanaticism. While the historic links with the Jewish and Muslim worlds offer more in common there is also a disturbing history of troubled relationships. The Catholic and Orthodox churches are also developing and strengthening links on common issues such as development and conservation with other major faiths such as Buddhism.

LAY MOVEMENTS

The Second Vatican Council (1962–65) reemphasized the role of laypeople in the Catholic Church to overcome the misconception that members of the clergy are the only important element in the church. The laity, or laypeople, are all those baptized Christians who have not been ordained into the threefold orders of the clergy. These orders are those of bishop, priest, and deacon. The role of the clergy is to administer the sacraments of the church. The role of the laity is to transform the world through the power of Christ that is communicated by these sacraments.

Since the Second Vatican Council lay communities have been formed, mostly in Europe, with special missions or goals. Some of them have moved on to other parts of the world. These laypeople carry on their ordinary lives in family and work but meet regularly for prayer and fellowship. These communities have distinctive orientations. The Focolare movement, for example, which began in Italy under the guidance of Chiara Lubich (1920–2008), is inspired by the Gospel, but its orientation is to promote unity among all peoples, Christians and non-Christians. Begun in Trent during the intense hatreds fostered by World War II, it aimed at promoting love and unity in the midst of anger and hatred. It has developed a spirituality promoting unity and has spread to other countries, first in Europe and then throughout the world.

The Catholic Church also has significant lay movements that challenge the current teachings of the church on issues such as the ordination of women, the celibacy of priests, and contraception. For example, in many parts of Europe the "We are the Church" movement has challenged the church hierarchy at least to explore these issues. The Catholic Church, however, has not been very responsive to these discussions.

THE COMMUNITY OF SANT' EGIDIO

The Community of Sant' Egidio began in Italy. Sant' Egidio is a parish church in Rome, where, in 1968, a group of high-school students wanted to take the Gospel more seriously. They formed a community that aimed to promote friendships with the poor, the elderly, immigrants, and the imprisoned to help them overcome loneliness, fear, and prejudice. It is a movement that has spread to 40,000 members in 60 countries and has had notable success in peacemaking efforts during the civil wars in Mozambique and Bosnia. Such movements are very much in accord with the efforts of the late Pope John Paul II and the present Pope Benedict XVI, who have attempted to encourage young people in particular to pursue a deeper form of spiritual life in a context where many view the Christian life as a mechanical performance of routine religious exercises.

THE PRIESTHOOD

Although the number of priests in some regions of the world has been increasing, it has dropped significantly among Catholic communities in the United States, Canada, western Europe, Australia, and elsewhere during the past 40 years. This has caused a serious shortage of pastors for Catholics in these lands. Many

Sister Salvinette, a sister of the Missionaries of Charity, teaching a catechism class in Saint Gabriel's Parish, southwest Detroit. This Catholic order, based in Kolkata (Calcutta), India, was founded in 1950 by Mother Teresa to work with the poor and to care for the dying. It now has communities on every continent and in most countries of the world.

parishes have had to be closed, and fewer masses are celebrated on Sundays and feast days. In the United States and Ireland the recent abuse scandals have lowered respect for priests, presenting the danger that calls to the priesthood might diminish even more. In its efforts to reverse the ill effects of these scandals the Catholic Church has most recently considered a review of seminary candidates and their training. In doing so one of the measures for seminary reform has focused on the official exclusion of homosexual candidates for the priesthood. This has raised in many circles the charge of injustice in locating the blame for the abuse scandals on homosexuals. Such a charge disturbs even more those who were already wounded and embarrassed by the abuse scandals themselves, and it lessens even more their respect for clerical church leaders.

It is in this atmosphere that much of the discussion concerning the priesthood turns today. How can the problem of the falling number of priests and the needs of the faithful be solved? Many suggestions have been made. One suggested solution is to do away with the obligation of celibacy and allow married priests: Many Orthodox priests are married, and even Eastern Rite Catholic priests are married. Why can the Catholic Church not follow suit? "Ordain women priests" is another suggestion: there are many Protestant ministers, and even Jewish rabbis, who are women. These religious groups changed their rules and some ask why the Catholic Church cannot do the same.

The late Pope John Paul II and the present Pope Benedict XVI have firmly opposed these solutions, citing tradition as their reason. A similar hard line is taken on the issue of the ordination of women, again citing tradition and a particular understanding of the fact that the Twelve Apostles were all men. The disappointment over women's ordinations touches many Catholics today, but there is currently no sign that the church will move in that direction. While the debate over the shortage of priests goes on, many parishes have opted for practical, acceptable, partial solutions. Many responsibilities that have traditionally been assumed by priests are no longer seen as necessarily priestly duties and have been taken over by laypeople.

CATHOLIC AND ORTHODOX VIEWS ON SEXUALITY AND ABORTION

The Catholic and Orthodox churches view sex as something naturally good. The primary purpose of sex is to produce children, if God grants this benefit, and to foster mutual love. The official attitude is that in the fostering of mutual love, sexual partners cannot by artificial means deliberately impede the natural goal of sexual union: the production of children. The Catholic prohibition against the use of condoms to prevent conception has come under even more intense criticism with the extensive spread of AIDS. Many, disagreeing, see condom use as the chief way to protect against contracting HIV.

The teaching of the churches regarding sexuality has many ramifications. Sexual union of unmarried persons is forbidden, since they are not in a formally committed relationship to raise the children who would be expected naturally to follow from their sexual union. Adultery, or sexual union with a person who is married to someone else, is forbidden for the same reasons.

HOMOSEXUALITY

Following the Catholic Church's sexual moral tradition, the Congregation for the Doctrine of the Faith has also strongly criticized efforts to portray homosexual unions as marriages. "Marriage is not just any relationship between human beings. It was established by the Creator with its own nature, essential properties, and purpose. No ideology can erase from the human spirit the certainty that marriage exists solely between a man and a woman, who by mutual personal gift, proper and exclusive to themselves, tend toward the communion of their persons. In this way, they mutually perfect each other, in order to cooperate with God in the procreation and upbringing of new human lives." Given this view of marriage, the church opposes homosexual unions as contrary to natural moral law and Christian tradition. At the same time the church insists that homosexual persons "must be accepted with respect, compassion and sensitivity. Every sign of unjust discrimination in their regard should be avoided." In contrast Orthodoxy does not debate this issue, nor does it feel necessary to pronounce, taking the position that silence is better than condemnation.

ABORTION

The Catholic Church's position on abortion has also raised many objections, especially in America and many western European countries. Often these challenges are once again made on the basis of the claim that freedom of choice is the chief component of human dignity. The Second Vatican Council, however, summarized the commitment of the Catholic Church to other values, such as the welfare of the fetus. It condemned abortion as an unspeakable crime and asked that the fetus be given the greatest care right from the moment of conception.

Although the various Orthodox churches are self-ruling and independent, they also remain strongly united in their common commitment to a moral life that is consistent with traditional Orthodox faith, and they also condemn many of the same forms of behavior that the Catholic Church does: abortion, euthanasia, disregard for human life, sexual immorality, and disintegration of the family.

THE CATHOLIC CHURCH AND ITS SOCIAL CHALLENGES

Much of the Catholic Church's involvement in social action movements was stimulated by the social encyclical letters of Pope Leo XIII (1878–1903): *Rerum Novarum* ("The Spirit of Revolutionary Change") and *Quadragesimo Anno* ("The Fortieth Year": a reconstruction of the social order). In these works he opposed socialism and in contrast gave the impulse for a reform of the social order in line with Christian principles.

These proclamations spurred the creation of Catholic schools, especially in the United States, to help poor immigrants and their children gain the educational background to advance in society. They also stimulated the spread of hospital care for the sick and the dying and their families, and they promoted the energies of priests and Catholic laypeople in the building of labor unions that brought workers better pay and better working conditions. Today the Catholic Church in various countries still fights, in more complicated circumstances, for the forgiveness of debt in poor nations and the establishment of laws to protect the poor and prevent the exploitation of underpaid workers. Since the Orthodox churches, especially in the United States, were originally made up of immigrant communities, they dedicated themselves to similar social missions on behalf of the poor.

VOICES OF SOCIAL CONCERN

The Second Vatican Council, heeding the voice of social concern sounded in the encyclical letters of Pope Leo XIII, called on

Catholics to become engaged in the modern world and its social problems. Since the social situations in many South and Central American countries was such that 90 percent of the people were counted among the poor, in 1968 the Catholic bishops of South America called on all Catholics to become involved in social issues. They also declared that the church should give special consideration, "a preferential option," to the poor.

LIBERATION THEOLOGY

In 1971 one of the responses to this call of the Catholic bishops found expression in *A Theology of Liberation* by Gustavo Gutierrez, a Peruvian priest, which began the movement called liberation theology. The chief characteristic of this movement is that it understands the church's Gospel message of freedom to be one that is interpreted in view of the experience of the poor and the oppressed, who are enslaved in different ways but especially by the social institutions under which they live.

In efforts to promote social justice the church, through many of its members, has moved into new and more delicate roles in different societies. Its judgments, discretion, prudence, and courage are tested in new and politically complicated ways. In recent years the late Pope John Paul II criticized a number of popular liberation theologians and their followers for becoming loosely associated and overidentified with political movements and promoting class warfare. Because of the *Instruction on Certain Aspects of the "Theology of Liberation"* (1984), a document published under the signature of Cardinal Ratzinger that is critical of certain positions of liberation theology, Ratzinger's election as Pope Benedict XVI has not been applauded by some liberation theologians. The Brazilian liberation theologian Leonardo Boff expressed his displeasure with the choice, and added: "I believe in miracles. Let's hope that Bene-

Orthodox monasteries built on the slopes of Mount Athos. One distinctive feature in Orthodoxy has been the revival of monasticism. In the 1960s places such as Mount Athos, the peninsula in the north of Greece that is entirely run by monks, was in danger of having to close because so few monks attended the 20 monasteries. Today there is a waiting list for people to join; a similar situation exists in countries such as Russia.

dict XVI becomes again the theologian I used to respect, who elicited hope, not fear."

THE ORTHODOX CHURCH AND ITS CHALLENGES

The Orthodox churches have had to respond in the last few decades to the collapse of communism and the rise of militant Islam. The collapse of communism has meant the rebuilding of shattered communities, churches, and moral standards in countries such as Russia and Georgia. As the patriarch of Moscow said in 1990, the coming of freedom was as severe a test of the church as the years of persecution under communism because "when we were persecuted, no one expected us to be able to help them. Now they want us to do everything!"

In the Middle East, the combination of reduced vocations to the priesthood, loss of members, and the rise of Islam has resulted in declining numbers of Oriental Orthodox communities. These political and social pressures have, however, seen an increase in the number of Orthodox Christians migrating from the Middle East to the United States and thereby strengthening American Orthodox communities.

CHALLENGES FOR THE AMERICAN ORTHODOX CHURCHES

The Orthodox churches in the United States have some special challenges of their own. These churches in many cases are strongly anchored in particular ethnic cultures. Traditionally this has made it difficult for them to develop harmony with one another. Each church has ties with its particular national and political background. Since their national traditions in

CHALLENGES FOR THE ORIENTAL ORTHODOX CHURCHES

The Oriental Orthodox churches are suffering in much the same way as the Catholic Church through loss of members and vocations to the priesthood and the monastic orders. This is exacerbated by the rise of Islam within the Middle East, which has led to many historic Christian communities seeing their young migrate to the United States and elsewhere. The war in Iraq, for example, has led to many Christians fleeing the country, while the rise of militant Islam in Egypt has created problems for the Coptic Church. The increasing numbers of Orthodox who have migrated to the United States has strengthened the existing Orthodox presence there, and it is possible that within a few years the heartland, numerically, of the ancient Orthodox churches of the Middle East will have shifted to the United States. The consequences of this will be considerable in terms of continuity, lifestyle, and leadership.

the old world often were opposed to one another's, historical memory has often kept them opposed in their new homeland. In particular instances the ethnic unity within these churches at first was beneficial: It brought a certain strength to each ethnic and religious church. These churches helped their Orthodox immigrants find support and identity in the United States. As the younger generations have become more Americanized, however, it has become more difficult to preserve close links to a church that has strong ties to an ethnic tradition. To meet these challenges efforts have been made to introduce English into the Divine Liturgy and to update music. Yet the traditions in these religious communities seem to be so strong that adaptation comes slowly.

Catholic lay missionaries working on a community project with AIDS orphans in the Korogocho slum, Nairobi, Kenya.

CONCLUSION

Throughout the long centuries of their existence the Catholic and Orthodox churches have had to face many challenges from within and without: persecutions, betrayals, schisms, and heresies. One can read about these events as early as the Acts of the Apostles and the Letters of Saint Paul. They are appreciated in our world today for the religious energy they bring to many people who continue, guided by the Gospel, to feed the hungry, give drink to the thirsty, and clothe the naked. They bring strong voices of hope to many throughout the world. They play leading roles in promoting peace and harmony among peoples. Each of these churches in its own way preaches high ideals for marriage and family life, for communal worship, and for eternal truths about God and human beings, about human weakness and sinfulness, and about the keys to salvation and redemption.

However, these churches also face stiff challenges in preaching and living the Gospel. The message they preach may seem lofty, and to modern ears it may appear naive, dreamy, and even disturbing. The Gospel life does not find its fulfillment in the unending list of material comforts advertised daily in newspapers and on television. In a world of quick solutions, immediate gratifications, and worth tied to salary and position, the Gospel message and way of life is often unwelcome, and so are the churches that preach and attempt to live it.

The Catholic Church and Orthodox churches have long memories, strong traditions, and long-range visions. They claim to be founded by Christ, whose kingdom was not of this world. They therefore follow the command of Christ: "Go, therefore, and make disciples of all nations . . . teaching them to obey everything that I have commanded you." (Matthew 28:18) These churches do not measure themselves and their successes according to human judgments. For them, God alone is the judge.

FACT FILE

Worldwide Numbers
There are approximately 1.1 billion Catholics and 220 million Orthodox Christians in the world.

Holy Symbol
There are many Christian symbols, most of which are based on the cross on which Jesus was executed (crucified). This "Chi-Rho" or Christogram symbol consists of the intersection of the capital Greek letters Chi (X) and Rho (P), which are the first two letters of "Christ" in Greek (ΧΡΙΣΤΟΣ, Christos).

Holy Writings
The Bible, consisting of the Old Testament of Judaism written in Hebrew, and the New Testament, originally written in Greek.

Holy Places
Israel is seen as important for its relation to the life of Jesus, and the Vatican City in Rome, seat of the pope, is a focal point for the Catholic Church.

Founders
Christianity, including Protestantism, Catholicism, and Orthodoxy, is named after Jesus of Nazareth—called "Christ" from the Greek word for "chosen one"—who was crucified in about 29 C.E.

Festivals
The major festivals include: Christmas, celebrating the birth of Jesus Christ (December 25); Easter, marking his death and resurrection (March–April); Ascension Day, celebrating his return to heaven (May); and Pentecost, which celebrates the coming of the Holy Spirit to his disciples (May–June).

BIBLIOGRAPHY

Bartholomew. *Encountering the Mystery: Understanding Orthodox Christianity Today.* New York: Doubleday, 2008.

Camille, Alice L. *Invitation to Catholicism: Beliefs, Teachings, Practices.* Chicago, Ill.: ACTA Publications, 2001.

Flinn, Frank K., and J. Gordon Melton. *Encyclopedia of Catholicism.* Encyclopedia of World Religions. New York: Checkmark Books, 2008.

Hill, Brennan. *The Ongoing Renewal of Catholicism.* Winona, Minn.: Saint Mary's Press, 2008.

Marty, Martin E. *A Short History of American Catholicism.* Allen, Tex.: Thomas More, 1995.

Pennock, Michael. *This Is Our Church: A History of Catholicism.* Notre Dame, Ind.: Ave Maria Press, 2007.

FURTHER READING

Beinert, Wolfgang, and Francis Schüssler Fiorenza. *Handbook of Catholic Theology.* New York: Crossroad, 1995.

Breck, John. *The Sacred Gift of Life: Orthodox Christianity and Bioethics.* Crestwood, N.Y.: St. Vladimir's Seminary Press, 2000.

Fahey, Michael A. *Orthodox and Catholic Sister Churches: East Is West and West Is East.* The Père Marquette lecture in theology, 1996. Milwaukee: Marquette University Press, 1996.

Florensky, Pavel, and Donald Sheehan. *Iconostasis.* Crestwood, N.Y.: St. Vladimir's Seminary Press, 2000.

Glazier, Michael, and Monika Hellwig. *The Modern Catholic Encyclopedia.* Collegeville, Minn.: Liturgical Press, 2004.

Gutirrez, Gustavo. *A Theology of Liberation.* Maryknoll, N.Y.: Orbis Books, 1988.

Maloney, George A. *Gold, Frankincense, and Myrrh: An Introduction to Eastern Christian Spirituality.* New York: Crossroads Pub. Co, 1997.

Sobrino, Jon. *The Principle of Mercy: Taking the Crucified People from the Cross.* Maryknoll, N.Y.: Orbis Books, 1994.

Stravinskas, Peter M. J. *Our Sunday Visitor's Catholic Encyclopedia.* Huntington, Ind.: Our Sunday Visitor Pub, 1998.

Vasileios, and Elizabeth Brière. *Hymn of Entry: Liturgy and Life in the Orthodox Church.* Contemporary Greek theologians, 1. Crestwood, N.Y.: St. Vladimir's Seminary Press, 1998.

WEB SITES

Further facts and figures, history, and current status of the religion can be found on the following Web sites:

www.catholic.org
This site gives the largest and broadest coverage of Catholics worldwide, with access to educational and news information about Catholicism.

www.newadvent.org
One of the biggest Catholic resources on the Internet. It has links to sites giving information on many aspects of Christian beliefs and Catholicism.

www.orthodoxinfo.com
Information on Orthodox Christianity worldwide.

www.americancatholic.org
This site provides the online editions of many American Catholic magazines and journals for people of all ages.

www.vatican.va
The official Vatican Web site, giving comprehensive information and images of the Vatican and its collections.

www.orc.org
The Web site of the Orthodox Church in America. It provides news, comments, and information.

GLOSSARY

apostle—One of the 12 disciples chosen by Jesus (Matthew 2:4) or certain other early Christian leaders (Acts 14:14; Romans 16:7; Galatians 1:1).

apostolate—The particular or special mission of a person or group who promotes one of their church's goals.

baptism—Ceremony in which one enters the church family. It is a way of showing that you have been washed free of sin by the death and rising from the dead of Jesus Christ.

basilica—A church, such as the Lateran Basilica, built according to an ancient Roman plan for a court of justice or a place of public assembly, with an oblong nave and a semicircular apse at one end.

catechism—A textbook regarding Christian beliefs and life used for preparing believers to accept the responsibilities of mature faith.

chrism—Holy oil blessed for confirmation and symbolizing the strength that is necessary for leading a mature Christian life and facing the challenges that the call to Christian maturity brings.

creed—A short statement of the basic beliefs of the Christian church (e.g., the Apostles' Creed, the Athanasian Creed, and the Nicene Creed).

Ecumenical Council—A worldwide council of the church called to settle important disputes of doctrine and discipline.

ecumenism—From the Greek *oikoumene*, "the whole inhabited world." Any attempts to deal with the relations between different Christian groups, or to think of ways in which divisions might be overcome.

Eucharist—The sacrament whereby the bread and wine become the body and blood of Christ.

excommunication—The formal cutting off of a person from the life of the church and the reception of the sacraments.

fathers of the church—Early church authors (e.g., Ambrose, Jerome, Augustine, Basil, Gregory of Nyssa) who explained the scriptures with great acuity and whose writings thus gained authority within the church community.

hymn—A religious poem set to music and sung as part of worship.

iconostasis—A screen, ornamented with rows of icons, that separates the nave from the altar in many Eastern churches. It is beyond this screen that the bread and wine are transformed into the body and blood of Christ during the Divine Liturgy.

Incarnation—The mystery believed by Christians that God became man by the union of the divine and human natures in the person of Jesus Christ.

indulgence—The removal in full or in part of the punishment due to sins already confessed and forgiven.

infallibility—The belief held by Roman Catholics that the pope cannot make an error in matters of faith and morals when he speaks by virtue of his office.

monk—A religious man following the Rule of Saint Benedict or the Orthodox rules and structures, who spends most of his day in prayer and who attempts to lead a perfect Christian life by taking vows pledging himself to poverty, chastity, and obedience.

novena—Roman Catholic devotions consisting of prayers or services held on nine consecutive days or weeks honoring Mary, the mother of Jesus, or the saints.

Pentecost—The feast celebrated by Christian believers, commemorating Christ's sending of the Holy Spirit to the apostles. It is considered by Christians to be the birthday of the church.

resurrection—The belief that Christ rose from the dead after his crucifixion and death. It is the guarantee, according to Saint Paul, that the followers of Christ will similarly survive physical death and be joined with their heavenly father.

Roman Curia—The group that serves as the pope's administrative arm. It consists of the secretariat of state, which assists the pope most directly in governing the church, and a number of other departments, each of which has a specific function.

sacraments—Signs of divine help or grace, needed for living a good Christian life, through which God confers the help of grace he promises.

schism—A split between two churches that does not involve the denial of any truth of the faith. Such a denial of a truth of the Christian faith would be called heresy.

Second Vatican Council—A worldwide church council for Roman Catholics opened by Pope John XXIII in 1962 for bringing Roman Catholic life and teaching up to date. Vatican II was closed by Pope Paul VI in 1965.

seminary—A school for training members of the clergy for the Roman Catholic and Eastern Orthodox churches.

Trinity—The Christian belief that in God there are three persons: the Father, the Son (who became man in Christ), and the Holy Spirit.

INDEX

lawgiver 33; resurrection of 38–39, 43, 77; suffering 33–34
Jesus prayer 67
Jewish people 17, 29–30, 42
John Paul II, Pope (1978–2005) 18, 64, 71, 72, 122, 127, 129
John the Baptist 31
Judas Iscariot 33, 35

K

Knights Templar 58

L

Last Supper 34–35, 86
lay movements 128–129
Lent 81–85, 101
liberation theology 134–135
literature 112–114
liturgy *See* Divine Liturgy; mass
Locke, John (1632–1704) 61
Luther, Martin (1483–1546) 59

M

marriage 88–90
martyrs 45
Mary, mother of Jesus 78–79
mass 13–14, 20, 25, 61, 79, 85–86, 87
Medieval Inquisition 57–58
Men, Father Alexander (1935–90) 21
Messiah *See* Jesus Christ
Methodius (ca. 825–85) 65–66
miracle plays 117
mission work 18, 21–23, 52
monasticism 48, 52–55, 60, 67, 101
Monophysites 47–48, 64, 93, 128
morality plays 117–118
Moses 33, 34
Mother Teresa (1910–97) 20
music 13, 110–112
mystery plays 116–117

N

Nestorianism 48, 50, 64
New Testament, the 26–27, 39; Acts 40–42, 98; Galatians 43–44; John 79, 98, 120; Luke 31, 37; Mark 31; Matthew 23, 30, 33–35, 37–39, 42, 95, 137
Nicene Creed, the 124
nuns 52, 53, 101

O

Old Testament 17, 39; Genesis 28–29; Isaiah 37; Ten Commandments 26, 28–29, 33
organization of the church 90–95
Oriental Orthodox churches 48, 93–95, 135
original sin 76–77

P

pagans 103
papacy *See* popes
Pascal, Blaise (1623–62) 99
passion plays 118–119
penance 88
persecution 45, 57–58, 61, 70
Pharisees 33, 34
Plainsong 110
popes 18, 51–52, 55–56, 57, 60–61, 62–63, 64, 71, 72–73, 90–92, 122–123, 126–127, 133, 134–135
prayer 52, 79, 85; The Hail Mary 77; the Jesus Prayer 67
priesthood 90, 129–131

R

reconciliation 88
reformation 59–61, 109
requiem mass 111–112
resurrection of Christ 38–39, 43, 77

rites of passage: baptism 58, 86–87; confirmation 87–88; funerals 111–112; marriage 88–90
Roman Curia 91
Rome 50, 51, 53, 55, 64
Rousseau, Jean-Jacques (1712–78) 62
Russian Orthodox Church 10, 68

S

saints 10, 24, 53, 54, 77–79, 80, 102, 103
scribes 33, 34
scriptures *See* Bible
Second Coming, the 81
seven sacraments 86–90
sex, the churches' views on 131–132
social issues 63–64, 133–135
Society of Jesus 61
Spanish Inquisition 58

T

Ten Commandments 26, 28–29, 33
theater 114–119
Twelve Apostles 33, 34–37, 39, 40–41, 44

W

Waldensians 58
"We are the Church" movement 129
women, ordination of 131
works of mercy 19, 25, 63–64, 133–134
World Council of Churches 125

Z

Zwingli, Ulrich (1484–1531) 59

ABOUT THE AUTHORS

Stephen F. Brown is chairperson of the theology department at Boston College. He has edited several volumes on medieval philosophy and theology, including *Philosophical Writings* by William of Ockham and *On Faith and Reason* by St. Thomas Aquinas.

Khaled Anatolios is associate professor of historic and systematic theology at the Weston Jesuit School of Theology and a specialist in Greek Patristic Theology.

ABOUT THE SERIES EDITORS

Martin Palmer is the founder of ICOREC (International Consultancy on Religion, Education, and Culture) in 1983 and is the secretary-general of the Alliance of Religions and Conservation (ARC). He is the author of many books on world religions.

Joanne O'Brien has an M.A. degree in theology and has written a range of educational and general reference books on religion and contemporary culture. She is co-author, with Martin Palmer and Elizabeth Breuilly, of *Religions of the World* and *Festivals of the World* published by Facts On File Inc.

PICTURE CREDITS